A Time of War

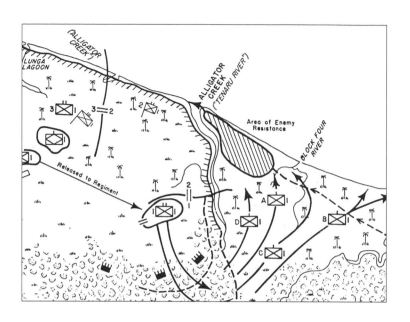

A Time of War

Remembering Guadalcanal, A Battle without Maps

William H. Whyte

With an introduction by James C. Bradford

Fordham University Press
New York
2000

Library of Congress Cataloging-in-Publication Data

Whyte, William Hollingsworth.
    A time of war: remembering Guadalcanal, a battle without
maps / William H. Whyte.
        p. cm.
    Includes bibliographical references and index.
    ISBN 0-8232-2007-9 (hc)—ISBN 0-8232-2008-7 (pbk)
    1. Whyte, William Hollingsworth. 2. Guadalcanal
(Solomon Islands), Battle of, 1942–1943—Personal narratives,
American. 3. United States. Marine Corps—Biography.
4. Marines—United States—Biography. I. Title.

D767.98.W45 2000
940.54'26—dc21   00-025150

Printed in the United States of America
00 01 02 03 04 5 4 3 2 1
First Edition

Contents

Acknowledgments   vii

Preface   ix

Introduction by James C. Bradford   xiii

1   Getting Ready   1

2   Joining Up   11

3   Shipping Out   21

4   Making a Landing   27

5   Meeting the Enemy   37

6   Fighting the Enemy   46

7   Patrolling   53

8   Our Turn   63

9   Winding Down   81

10   Recuperating   88

11   Teaching   93

12   Thereafter   104

Appendix A: Hyakutake Meets the Marines   111

Appendix B: Pacific Fleet Chain of Command   139

Index   141

Acknowledgments

My wife, Jenny Bell, pulled the pieces of this book together. Chester Baum, Barbara Kerr, Albert LaFarge, and Susan St. John made valuable contributions. My stepbrother, James M. Perry, a veteran journalist, tracked down loose ends and helped in editing the final manuscript. I am indebted to all of them.

Preface

"Jesus wept!" the colonel roared. "Of course it's the Lunga River, Whyte, and no damn lieutenant is going to tell me it isn't. More of this kind of talk out of you and we're going to start thinking about a court-martial."

The man giving me hell was Lieutenant Colonel William N. "Wild Bill" McKelvy, commander of my outfit—the Third Battalion, First Marine Regiment, First Marine Division—and this was a fine pickle the two of us were in on August 7, 1942, on the first day of the first major counterattack on the ever-victorious Japanese army in World War II, all of it happening just eight months after the disaster at Pearl Harbor.

We were going to war without proper maps.

The First Marines' assignment after the initial unopposed landing on Guadalcanal was to move to the southwest in the direction of a hill called Mt. Austen. We would know we were getting close when we came to the Lunga River. The hill, our crude map showed, was close to the northern shoreline, and should be an easy march from the beach.

But it wasn't anything of the sort. Mt. Austen, we finally discovered, was six miles away, and our wretched map couldn't even tell us what features to look for. The going was rough. After fording a shallow stream called the Ilu River, we emerged into a plain of kunai grass, which was more than eight feet tall and trapped the heat mercilessly. Nor did the map tell us how steep the ridges were or the difficulties that made going up and down such a sore trial. I worried that the forty-two-year-old McKelvy, huffing and puffing, would topple over, but he plunged on. Toward dusk we began to hear rippling water, and soon enough we reached a riverbank. McKelvy had no doubt; this was the Lunga, and our destination, Mt. Austen, couldn't be far away.

I told him, no sir, it's the Ilu again, and that's when he began shouting about the possibility of a court-martial. There were so many "Jesus wepts" I wondered if that might not soon be my name, Jesus Wept Whyte. I pointed out that the stream was flowing to our left, and that the Lunga, when we did find it, would be flowing downhill toward the north coast. What we had been seeing was the Ilu, and we were nowhere near Mt. Austen.

Gravity stood confirmed.

A few days later, we received prints of the most recent aerial photos of the area in contention. You could see the trail of the First Marines etched in the tall kunai grass, where it had been flattened by our progress. And where did the trail end? At the Ilu, of course. McKelvy offered no apology, not then, not ever, for anything.

We never did sort out the names of these rivers and streams, with the Ilu eventually becoming confused with the larger Tenaru. It became so mixed up that by the time the fighting was over even the natives on the island were confused as to which was which.

I was young—twenty-five years old—and I not only had no doubt we were seeing the Ilu again but also the temerity to challenge McKelvy's belief that it was the Lunga. McKelvy was part of the peacetime Marine Corps, the son of a Marine, a graduate of the Naval Academy at Annapolis. Like his father, he had put in time with the Marines in Haiti. McKelvy came from the "Old Breed," when the Corps was barely larger than the New York Police Department. He was proud and stubborn, and learning to read maps had never been part of his preparation for war. I don't doubt he resented the thousands of us, the "New Breed," flowing into his outfit and changing it forever.

We were together for four months, from August 7 until, sick and exhausted, we were relieved by soldiers on December 15. They were to be the most exciting four months of my life.

A Note on Sources

This book is based upon my own papers in the Marine Corps Historical Center at the Washington Navy Yard. These papers include all of the translated interviews with Japanese prisoners and all the excerpts from Japanese diaries that I mention in the book. I used these papers in my lectures during World War II at the Marine Corps Staff and Command School,

Quantico, Virginia. The articles I wrote for the Marine Corps *Gazette,* growing out of my lectures, can also be found among my papers. The papers also contain the letters I wrote from Guadalcanal to my father, William H. Whyte, Sr., and my stepmother, Margaret.

I have also drawn from the papers of my regimental commander, Clifton B. Cates, including his unpublished book of memoirs, also located at the Marine Corps Historical Center.

A key to any understanding of our role on Guadalcanal is the exceptionally candid book *The Memoirs of General Alexander A. Vandegrift, USMC* (New York: Norton, 1964), written by our commanding general and Robert B. Asprey.

It would be difficult to single out a better unit history than the one written by my old friend George McMillan, *The Old Breed: A History of the First Marine Division in World War II* (Washington, D.C.: Infantry Journal Press, 1949).

The Marine Corps has published one major work, *History of U.S. Marine Corps Operation in World War II: Pearl Harbor to Guadalcanal,* by Lieutenant Colonel Frank O. Hough, Major Verle E. Ludwig, and Henry I. Shaw, Jr., and two valuable monographs on the campaign, *First Offensive: The Marine Campaign for Guadalcanal,* by Henry I. Shaw, Jr., and *The Guadalcanal Campaign,* by Major John L. Zimmerman.

I have drawn from time to time from the official *Final Report on the Guadalcanal Operation, Phases I through V,* and Samuel E. Morison's *The Struggle for Guadalcanal: History of United States Naval Operations in World War II,* vol. 5 (Boston: Little, Brown, 1950). I have relied on Robert D. Heinl's *Soldiers of the Sea: The United States Marine Corps, 1775-1962* (Baltimore: The Nautical and Aviation Publishing Company of America, 1991), a workmanlike history of the Marine Corps.

Though it is clearly the definitive account of the campaign, Richard B. Frank's impressive book *Guadalcanal* (New York: Penguin, 1992) sometimes seems to skip over the accomplishments of the Third Battalion, First Marines. McKelvy would have been livid.

W. H. W.

Introduction

James C. Bradford

William H. Whyte is most often remembered by the general public as the author of *The Organization Man,* the 1956 best-selling examination of modern American society.[1] Urbanologists remember him as a student of urban behavior and designer of living spaces. He was both, of course, but first he was a Marine, a fact he paid homage to when he said on the dust jacket of *The Organization Man* that he "was educated at Princeton and in the United States Marine Corps at Guadalcanal."

Whyte was born in West Chester, Pennsylvania, on October 1, 1917. The son of a railroad executive, he enjoyed his upbringing in the Brandy-wine Valley, at his grandmother's home on Cape Cod, and at St. Andrew's School in Middletown, Delaware. It was at St. Andrew's that Whyte began his writing career, serving as editor of the school newspaper. After graduation in 1935, Holly, as he was known to friends, entered Princeton University. Majoring in English, he served on the editorial staff of the *Nassau Lit,* and wrote a prize-winning play, but gave little thought to a literary career. Instead he joined the Vick Chemical Company and trained for a career in marketing. After only two years Whyte decided that selling Vicks Vapo-Rub and other products was not for him and enlisted in the Marine Corps. It was October 1941. World War II raged in Europe and Asia and threatened to engulf America. Even with war on the horizon the Marine Corps remained a small and, as Whyte believed, elite force. The young officer candidate took pride in the hard training and indoctrination into Marine Corps lore. Whyte reveled in the loyalty to the Corps exhibited by

Marines both then and fifty years later. With pride he quotes Brute Krulak in *A Time of War:* "A Marine believes in his God, in his country, in his
Corps, in his buddies, and in himself."

It is ironic that a decade after leaving the Corps in 1945, Whyte would
devote three years to analyzing the factors that led men—and their wives—
to give their allegiance to large nonmilitary organizations, including
churches, research laboratories, medical societies, and universities, but
most importantly to business corporations. He concluded that a new
"Social Ethic" was replacing the "Protestant Ethic" of self-reliance, ambi-
tion, and individualism. The Protestant Ethic legitimized resistance to
large-scale organizations, but the new Social Ethic made such groups the
source of creativity as well as of comfort and conformity. Whyte counseled
resistance to pressures within organizations that stifle individual thought
and reduce their members to a common denominator via the "tyranny
of the majority." "In our attention to making the organization work we
have come close to deifying it," he warned.

Some of the same characteristics that attracted Whyte to the Marine
Corps repelled him when he found them in large corporations. Whyte's
Organization Man would join David Riesman's dissection of urban middle-class values in *The Lonely Crowd;* John Kenneth Galbraith's critique of
corporate America in *American Capitalism;* Sloan Wilson's condemnation
of corporate conformity in *The Man in the Gray Flannel Suit;* C. Wright
Mills's indictment of the American political system in *The Power Elite;* and
Vance Packard's exposé of the manipulation of consumers by advertisers
in *The Hidden Persuaders* in their negative assessments of modern American society as well as in deploring the conformity of the 1950s.[2]

Like most of these writers, Whyte examined the lives not of the poor or
disadvantaged, but of the middle class, and acknowledged the improved
standard of living made available to most Americans by the efficiencies of
corporations and other large institutions.[3] He believed that economic pros-
perity was permanent, that the United States was becoming an overwhelm-
ingly middle-class society, and that class antagonism would soon be a thing
of the past. Thus Whyte concluded that the challenges of the future would
not be physical ones—poverty, health care, and social ills that could be dealt
with by political action—but problems of the psyche and spirit.

The manuscript for *The Organization Man* grew out of interviews and
research that Whyte conducted for a series of articles published in *Fortune*
magazine, his employer since June 1946, shortly following his discharge
from the Marine Corps. In *The Organization Man,* Whyte focused on the

centralization of power in large organizations. He did not condemn huge corporations, governmental agencies, law firms, research laboratories, foundations, or universities per se, but his descriptions of these "self-perpetuating institutions" and their denizens are hardly positive. Instead of concentrating on the institutions themselves, offering alternative forms of organization, or suggesting specific remedies to their ills, Whyte focused on "the personal impact that organization life has had on the individuals within it." He warned about the stifling effect that an overemphasis on functioning within an organization and "fitting in" as a member of a team could have on individual creativity and initiative. Still, he did not suggest that his readers rebel against the organization, but instead he counseled them to strive to understand the organization in which they worked so that they could work more effectively within it and use it to their own advantage.[4]

Whyte did not draw a distinction between the needs of a society in times of war and peace, though he may have considered such delineation self-evident to his readers. He was content to describe what he observed and to ponder its implications without seeking the origin of such behavior. Nowhere does he indicate that the leaders of the institutions he criticizes had learned the value of organization and teamwork during World War II, often as members of the armed forces, and that organization and teamwork made a vital contribution to Allied victory. Indeed, victory in World War II came at least as much from "the organization man" as from the rugged individual exercising personal initiative. Harold Kirby Taylor, Whyte's classmate at Officers Candidate School (OCS), is a fine example of what Whyte would later call an "organization man." When Whyte described him to students at his old boarding school, he said that Taylor did not just follow the other students at OCS, but "stuck his neck out [and lectured Whyte and other officer candidates] incessantly on our somewhat lackadaisical attitude toward the military profession." At the time, Whyte and his group "were amused" by Taylor's "spit and polish[, his] strict discipline," and his adherence to the letter of Marine Corps regulations and dubbed Taylor "Ramrod." Whyte admits that he did not appreciate the value of being such an "organization man" during OCS, but he testified that Taylor's methods paid off on Guadalcanal, where Taylor "died a hero." In retrospect Whyte paid tribute to Taylor, calling him "one hell of a Marine."

While *The Organization Man* was in press, Whyte began studying the problems connected to the decline of central cities and the rise of suburbs. First presented in articles published in *Fortune*, his views reached a wider audience when reprinted in *The Exploding Metropolis* (1958).[5] Whyte's writings brought him to the attention of Laurance S. Rockefeller, who became his patron and provided funding for many of Whyte's projects.[6]

This backing helped make it possible for Whyte to leave *Fortune* in 1958 and embark on a new career as an observer of city life. For sixteen years he filmed pedestrians, sat in parks and talked with people, and studied strip malls (he despised them) and parking lots to learn how people interacted in public spaces. The result was a series of books in which he decried the "fortressing" of American cities, advocated creating more open spaces, and called for fewer restrictions on their use. His work buttressed the movement led by Jane Jacobs to block construction of superhighways across 125th, 59th, and 34th Streets, which would have fundamentally changed Manhattan. Whyte loved large cities, especially New York, where he would spend his last fifty years. For him city streets formed "the river of life . . . where we come together."[7]

The corporate and urban jungles of late-twentieth-century America were far from those of Guadalcanal, which had provided a "coming of age" for Holly Whyte. Following Officers Candidate School at Quantico, Virginia, the twenty-four-year-old second lieutenant reported to the First Marine Division at New River, North Carolina. There Whyte and his fellow "ninety-day wonders" learned as much from the veteran sergeants as did the young privates who had recently completed boot camp at Parris Island, South Carolina. The war was not going well in the Pacific, and there was little time to prepare the First Marines for combat.

The Japanese attacked Pearl Harbor while Whyte was still at Quantico. In January 1942 Japanese forces occupied Rabaul on New Britain and began developing the complex of bases that would serve as their citadel in the Southwest Pacific. In March the Japanese expanded their operations to the north coast of New Guinea. Allied forces were reeling from Burma to the Philippines, where the last American troops surrendered on May 6. Three days earlier, on May 3, Japan sent troops ashore on Tulagi to establish a seaplane base at the southern end of the Solomon Islands.[8] At precisely the same time, American and Japanese naval forces searched for each other in the Coral Sea south of Tulagi and Guadalcanal. Shortly after midnight on May 4, Rear Admiral Frank Fletcher received news of the Japanese landing at Tulagi in the Solomons from an Australian-based aircraft and ordered his Task Force 17 to set course for the area. Within striking distance at daybreak, Fletcher launched the first of three attacks against Tulagi and nearby Gavutu. Aircraft from the *Yorktown* (CV-5) dropped twenty-two torpedoes and seventy-six 1,000-pound bombs that destroyed five seaplanes and sank a destroyer, three minecraft, and four barges at a cost of three U.S. aircraft. Turning northeastward, Fletcher recovered his aircraft, altered course to the southward, and circled back westward to link up with other Allied forces. On May 7 and 8 aircraft from U.S. and Japanese carriers located and engaged their enemy. The Japanese sank the aircraft carrier *Lexington* (CV-2), the oiler *Neosho* (AO-23), and the destroyer *Sims* (DD-409) and damaged the *Yorktown*. Japan lost the *Shoho,* a smaller carrier than the *Lexington,* and two of its other carriers—*Shokaku* and *Zuikaku*—were damaged. Thus the Japanese won a tactical victory by sinking more tonnage than they lost, but it was a strategic victory for the United States because the Japanese invasion force that was headed for Port Moresby in New Guinea was forced to turn back. A month later the United States won a decisive victory against the Japanese at Midway, sinking four of their aircraft carriers while losing only one of its own. The victories at Coral Sea and Midway made it possible for American planners to consider launching an offensive for the first time in the war.

Out in the war zone, General Douglas MacArthur, Commander-in-Chief Southwest Pacific Area, and Admiral Chester Nimitz, Commander-in-Chief Pacific Ocean Areas, agreed that a counteroffensive should be opened as quickly as possible. MacArthur preferred to strike directly at Rabaul, while Nimitz thought that Tulagi should be the first target. In Washington, Admiral Ernest J. King had favored an offensive in the Southwest Pacific since February, but the invasion of North Africa planned for November 1942 had priority for men and supplies. When it became clear that operations could be undertaken with the forces and supplies already assigned to the Pacific, the other members of the Joint Chiefs of Staff agreed to a limited offensive with the strategic objective of blocking further advances by the Japanese. On June 23 and 24 Admiral King alerted Nimitz that plans were being made for the seizure of Tulagi. On June 24 General MacArthur informed Marshall that the Navy's line of attack was acceptable, and a day later occupation of the Santa Cruz Islands was added to the objectives of the operation. All that remained to settle was the question of overall command. It took a week to hammer out a compromise under which the initial attack would be commanded by a naval officer but once Tulagi was occupied command would shift to MacArthur as commander of the Southwest Pacific Area. On July 2, 1942, the Joint Chiefs ordered that operations begin with the seizure of Tulagi and the Santa Cruz Islands, east of the Solomons. With MacArthur busy in New Guinea and King unwilling to transfer naval forces to

MacArthur's command, the Joint Chiefs decided to shift the boundary between the Pacific and Southwest Pacific Areas westward to 159 degrees so that the eastern Solomons, including Guadalcanal and Tulagi, would come within the Pacific Area. Nimitz would be in overall command from Hawaii with Vice Admiral Robert L. Ghormley, his deputy for the South Pacific Area, exercising strategic command. Under Ghormley, Vice Admiral Fletcher would have tactical command of the Expeditionary Force, Rear Admiral Richmond Kelly Turner would command the Amphibious Force, and Major General Alexander A. Vandegrift would command Marine Corps forces once they were ashore.[9]

Nimitz had begun planning such an operation prior to receipt of the directive from Washington. On July 5 he was meeting with Admiral King in San Francisco when an intelligence report arrived from Pearl Harbor saying that a Japanese naval party, including pioneer forces, had landed on Guadalcanal. From this information analysts concluded that the enemy planned to construct an airfield on the island. They feared that the establishment of such base might presage a thrust southeastward that would sever the line of communications between the United States and Australia, and plans were quickly changed to focus the counteroffensive on the seizure of Guadalcanal and Tulagi.[10]

Meanwhile, Holly Whyte and the First Marine Division made their way to New Zealand, the lead elements arriving in its capital, Wellington, in mid-June. When the division left Hawaii, its commander, General Vandegrift, thought he would have six months to train his troops before committing them to combat, but on June 26 he learned that he would have only four weeks to plan operations, reload his cargo ships, and conduct a hasty practice landing on Koro in the Fiji Islands. Only about one-third of the First Division Marines actually participated in the landing portion of the rehearsal, an exercise Vandegrift later called "a complete bust." Colonel Clifton B. Cates, a regimental commander, bemoaned the lack of training. He said that from the time his unit was formed until it entered combat, it "had less than three months of battalion training. Not once [did we have] a regimental problem, much less training with planes, tanks, and other units."[11]

On the last day of July the First Division set sail for Guadalcanal. With 19,514 officers and men, the division was subdivided into three infantry regiments, one artillery and one engineer regiment, and a division headquarters battalion. Each infantry regiment had 3,168 men divided into a headquarters company, a weapons company, and three battalions. Each battalion of 933 Marines had a headquarters company, a weapons company, and three rifle companies. Whyte served in the headquarters company of the Third Battalion, First Marines, one of the regiments comprising the First Marine Division. He was an intelligence officer but with little information about the area—even Allied maps on Guadalcanal were inaccurate.[12] Whyte had only an inkling of what was in store for the Marines when they landed on the north coast of the island on August 7, 1942. Planning for the campaign had been rudimentary at best. When elements of the First Marines, including Whyte's regiment, splashed ashore without opposition from the Japanese, they assumed it would be easy to seize their first objective, Mt. Austen. They soon learned the inadequacy of their maps when that objective proved to be several miles inland through eight-foot-tall kunai grass that trapped the heat and made even walking difficult.

What quickly developed on Guadalcanal was the first major test of ground combat strength between the United States and Japan. There had been previous fighting in the Philippines, but in that contest the Japanese had caught the American army unprepared. On New Guinea it was Australians, not Americans, who formed the bulk of the Allied forces fighting at best a holding action. Thus, the first offensive by Allied ground troops against the Japanese came in the Solomons at Guadalcanal and Tulagi. It was also the first American ground offensive of the war. The immediate goal was to seize the partially constructed Japanese airfield on Guadalcanal before it could be made operational, an objective quickly achieved. But rather than win the battle for Guadalcanal, the capture of the airfield simply marked the beginning of what developed into the Marines' longest campaign in World War II.

The battle for control of Guadalcanal and what Americans learned from it forms the heart of William Whyte's memoir, published here for the first time. In it Whyte has not altered his language to make it more acceptable to modern readers. In passages quoted from letters to members of his family the enemy remain "the Japs," as they were termed at the time. Whyte is nonchalant about events and does not overstate problems. He notes that the ships carrying the First Marine Division's supplies arrived in Wellington loaded for an "administrative" landing—that is, an unopposed landing utilizing port facilities—and that the cargo had to be offloaded onto the pier and then "combat loaded," with items needed first in battle on top. The First Marine Division arrived in Wellington on July 11, had only eleven days to accomplish the task, and did much of the reloading in the rain.[13]

In *A Time of War,* Whyte admits errors that he and other Americans committed, such as the time the patrol he led stopped for lunch and lay eating their rations and watching aircraft overhead without posting sentries or noticing they were close enough to an enemy battalion for it to have killed every American. This admission of his failure to take even elementary precautions when stopping for lunch forms part of his assessment of the strengths and weaknesses of both the Americans and their enemy. Whyte judges Japanese morale to be low, notes their "amazing lack of precautions taken for security"—American patrols often got within fifteen or twenty yards of the Japanese and were able to open fire first—and marvels at their failure to take advantage of favorable terrain to employ snipers. For their part, Americans were little better at mounting sentries and consistently made noise that betrayed their positions. Whyte is sharply critical of the failure of Japanese soldiers to retrieve and bury their dead.

Whyte is equally perceptive in his assessments of both American and Japanese officers. Senior Japanese leaders come in for much criticism. "The Japanese army was still basically designed for operations against the Chinese," Whyte notes, and it lacked the firepower needed "for action against the more powerfully armed American units." Japanese commanders on Guadalcanal compounded this organizational weakness by employing what artillery they possessed ineffectively and failing to competently support their infantry or to launch a serious artillery campaign against Henderson Field. Japanese generals never capitalized on their victories or pushed home the advantages gained thereby, thus giving Americans time to recover from their setbacks. Whyte is equally critical of Vice Admiral Fletcher for withdrawing his carriers to positions where they could not adequately support the Marines ashore on Guadalcanal, and of Rear Admiral Turner, whose "ink spot" strategy Whyte dismisses as "absolutely absurd" and whose ill-conceived insistence on construction of an airfield on swampland near Aolo Bay was only abandoned after two weeks of wasted work by Seabees and troops who were needed elsewhere.[14]

Lower-level commanders come in for their share of criticism. Among the Japanese, Whyte singles out "the egregious Colonel [Akinosuku] Oka" for his timidity and avoidance of battle. Whyte expressed respect for his own commander, Lieutenant Colonel William N. McKelvy, Jr., but he knew that McKelvy's strengths—persistence and the ability to inspire enlisted men—were offset by his rash glory-seeking when he volunteered his unit for a diversionary attack against the Japanese flank on October 8, by his inability to accept advice from subordinates, and by the fact that he was "mean to his staff [even though] all of them served him well." Indeed, the McKelvy described by Whyte is more a rugged individualist than a team player, even if he was an "organization man" in his respect for the Marine Corps.

On a more mundane level, Whyte observes that after two months in the field both sides suffered from tropical diseases, while neither possessed adequate maps, made good use of camouflage, exercised fire discipline, mounted adequate patrols, or posted sentries effectively. Whyte drew many of these conclusions from his analysis of captured Japanese diaries, part of his duties as an intelligence officer.

Any participant sees only a part of any campaign or battle, and Whyte has provided one of the few extant eyewitness accounts of the Japanese army's October 23 tank attack near the mouth of the Matanikau River. His battalion was responsible for the defense of that portion of the American lines. Its men fired 37mm anti-tank guns to destroy eight Japanese tanks, and Private Joseph D. R. Champagne used a grenade to disable another tank until a 75mm half-track could finish it off. This was the only Japanese tank action of the campaign, but it rarely receives as much coverage as other engagements, and never in the same detail provided by Whyte. The battle is noted in most accounts of combat on Guadalcanal, but only briefly, perhaps because none of the famous war correspondents who covered Guadalcanal was present to send a report to his newspaper or magazine in the United States or to include an eyewitness account in a book about Guadalcanal.[15]

As 1942 drew to a close the Second Marine Division and two army divisions, the Americal and the Twenty-fifth, began arriving on Guadalcanal. They were formed into the XIV Corps troops under the command of Army Major General Alexander Patch and on December 8 officially relieved the First Marines. A week later Whyte and the rest of the Third Battalion left Guadalcanal for Australia. The campaign for control of the island would continue for another two months. In the end, Guadalcanal proved to be the first decisive defeat suffered by the Japanese army. Its losses numbered 23,000 dead from battle and disease, compared to 1,598 American killed and 4,709 wounded. Of these 1,152 of the dead and 2,799 of the wounded were Marines. By capturing the airfield on Guadalcanal and the seaplane base at Tulagi, the Marines blocked Japanese expansion southeastward. By forcing Japan to commit resources to Guadalcanal, the Marines took pressure from MacArthur's army troops in New Guinea. Guadalcanal was not an end, but it was the beginning, both of the island-hopping campaign up the Solomon Islands and of the dual drive across the Pacific which resulted in total Allied victory over the Japanese three years to the month after Marines first landed on Guadalcanal.

For William Whyte, combat duty ended with his departure from Guadalcanal. Recurring bouts of malaria led to a fortnight in a hospital on Tasmania, followed in time by orders home to the United States along with other Marines who could not "shake that malaria bug." Returning to West Chester to recuperate, Whyte soon tired of the inactivity. In July 1943 he wrote to his old regimental commander, Colonel Cates, who was now a brigadier general commanding Marine Corps Schools at Quantico, and volunteered to become an instructor. Cates arranged for the transfer, and Whyte soon began teaching about the Guadalcanal campaign. He told his students that the Japanese could have won the campaign but that they threw victory away by underestimating the Americans and making elementary errors. Whyte contended that Vandegrift, the American commanding general, "outfought and outthought his enemy throughout the campaign."

While teaching at Quantico, Whyte wrote a series of articles for the *Marine Corps Gazette* to share his experiences with a wider audience. In "Throw Away the Book?" he relates the experiences of a mortar platoon in the Third Battalion, First Marines, his old outfit, to illustrate the value of mastering the principles of "'correct' procedure."[16] A month later he contributed "Observation vs. the Jap" to the same journal. In this article Whyte emphasized the value of individuals' working as a team to gather intelligence. "As in every Intelligence function it is not the individual report which counts, but the mass."[17]

Whyte left the Marine Corps in January 1945. In *A Time of War* he describes going to the offices of *Fortune* magazine, presenting copies of his writings for the *Marine Corps Gazette,* and being hired as a staff writer. He does not mention meeting Charles Edmundson, who was associate editor of the magazine, but one wonders if the two were acquainted. Both contributed articles to the *Marine Corps Gazette,* and they may have met during the war in the magazine's offices on 14th Street in Washington.[18]

One of Whyte's longest and most interesting articles appeared in the *Marine Corps Gazette* six months after he left the service. In "Hyakutake Meets the Marines" Whyte described the Guadalcanal campaign from the perspective of the Japanese. He stated that the article "is not intended to be a definitive [account], but is rather an attempt to reconstruct the actions of the Japs by 'reading between the lines' of their official communiques and propaganda broadcasts as measured against our own narratives of the campaign. Imagination has of necessity been used liberally, but while many of the events described are hypothetical, it is felt they are typical of the Jap as we have come to know him."[19] Over fifty years later the article remains of interest, particularly when its speculations are compared to Whyte's memoirs and to modern accounts such as Richard B. Frank's *Guadalcanal,* which examines the campaign from the perspective of both the Americans and the Japanese. In his memoir Whyte calls Frank's work "impressive," though he notes that it "sometimes seems to skip over the accomplishments of the Third Battalion, First Marines."

Whyte's final essays for the *Marine Corps Gazette* did not deal directly with Guadalcanal. "Outguessing the Enemy" advised intelligence officers and others to be pragmatic and focus their analyses on the enemy's capabilities, not his intentions, which are much harder to gauge. Japan's "much regretted decision to launch the Pearl Harbor attack was the result of paying too much attention to what the 'decadent' Americans probably would do, and too little to what they could do."[20] The same principle applies to tactical situations. In "Will the Queen Die?" Whyte cautioned that those who predict the demise of the infantryman, the "queen of battle," as a result of the development of guided missiles and atomic weapons would be proven wrong and that though "the soldier of the future may be a weird looking spectacle indeed . . . [h]e will still be an infantryman."[21] In his final, two-part article on "Information into Intelligence," Whyte again stressed the need for continuity in intelligence procedures. In the first installment, "Collation and Evaluation," he argued that "in spite of changing methods of warfare, intelligence fundamentals remain the same" and that the maintenance of an "up-to-date journal" and a "well-kept situation map" will be as vital in the future as they were in the past. In the second installment, "Interpretation and Dissemination," Whyte summed up the qualities of a good intelligence officer: "The transformation of information into intelligence requires no super-mind gifted with a mystical intuition, but one with sufficient humility not to short-cut sound procedure and jump to immediate conclusions. . . . Information must be recorded in a journal and put on the situation map, the item is classified by subject heading in the worksheet so that it may more easily be 'worked.'"[22]

Whyte's call for adherence to standard operating procedures and group norms at the end of World War II stands in sharp contrast to the views expressed in *The Organization Man* a decade later. The situations were obviously different—in 1945 and 1946 Whyte was a relatively young man writing from the perspective of a combat veteran in a just-completed war, while in 1955 he was a mature student of human nature writing as an observer of domestic institutions. Still, it would have been interesting to ask him if he believed that the criticisms he leveled in *The Organization Man* applied to military as well as civilian institutions, and in time of war as well as in time of peace. It is speculations such as these that make one wish to have known Holly Whyte personally.

On January 12, 1999, Whyte passed away at age eighty-one, still a resident of the New York City he studied and loved. He left America a better place for having lived here. He left also a corpus of writing that will provide future generations with insight into twentieth-century America—not the least part of that corpus is his memoir of service on Guadalcanal published here for the first time.

Whyte's experience as a writer is reflected in simple, direct, and concise prose with which he tells his story. Holly Whyte had an extraordinarily busy career, and he did not begin work on his memoir until the final months of his life. Given his prominence and the quality of his memoir, one may speculate that had Whyte found time to complete a longer manuscript, many publishers would have been pleased to offer it to the public. Instead, Whyte deferred work on the memoir until near the end of his life. The result is a history neither of the First Marines nor of the entire campaign on Guadalcanal.

In no way does Whyte attempt to be comprehensive or to speak for other Marines. His is a personal memoir, telling the story of his service in the Marine Corps with emphasis on his experiences on Guadalcanal. As such it invites comparison with works by others who were present during the battle for Guadalcanal: John Hersey, Richard Tregaskis, Herbert Christian Merillat, Robert Leckie, Thomas H. Gallant, Samuel B. Griffith II, Alexander Vandegrift, and Merrill B. Twining.[23]

Each writer had a unique perspective. The accounts by the journalists Tregaskis and Hersey were published while war still raged and thus were subject to censorship. Both cover a shorter time frame than Whyte. John Hersey's *Into the Valley* recounts a single patrol he accompanied on Guadalcanal. Such a limited scope allows him to describe events in vivid detail and to plumb the thoughts of the participants.[24] Tregaskis's *Guadalcanal Diary* covers a longer period. He linked up with the Marines in July, landed with them on August 7, and was present at the First Division command post during the battle at Bloody Ridge. Whyte undoubtedly met Tregaskis, since he mentions that his unit commander, McKelvy, was pleased to have been interviewed by the International News Service correspondent. He also quotes Tregaskis's *Guadalcanal Diary* several times in chapter six of *A Time of War*. Two weeks after that engagement, Tregaskis took off from Henderson Field in a B-17 for a reconnaissance mission over Bougainville. The plane did not return to Guadalcanal but continued on to another island from which Tregaskis flew to Hawaii. There he completed the manuscript for *Guadalcanal Diary* by the first week in November and sent it by airmail to New York, where it was immediately accepted for publication by Random House. Early in 1943 it appeared simultaneously in Canada and the United States and was a selection of the Book-of-the-Month Club.[25] Holly Whyte's memoir shares the "ground level" perspective of Hersey and Tregaskis, but covers a longer period and is that of a military participant, not a journalist observer.

Two journalists published accounts of their experiences as enlisted men on Guadalcanal. Robert Leckie, a reporter before the war, joined the Marine Corps shortly after the Japanese attack on Pearl Harbor. He served in the First Division as a machine gunner and scout and a decade after the war published a memoir that contains a particularly evocative account of night in the jungle:

> It was darkness without time. It was an impenetrable darkness. To the right and left of men rose up those terrible formless things of my imagination, which I could not see, but I dared not close my eyes lest the darkness crawl beneath my eyelids and suffocate me. . . . My ears became my being and I could hear the specks of life that crawled beneath my clothing. . . . I could hear the darkness gathering against me and the silences that lay between the moving things. I could hear the enemy everywhere about me, whispering to each other and calling my name. I lay open mouthed and half-mad beneath that giant tree. I had not looked into the foliage before the darkness and now I fancied it infested with Japanese.

Leckie, who later fought at Pelelieu, devoted eighty pages of his memoir to Guadalcanal.[26] Thomas Gallant, the other journalist and enlisted man with the Marines on Guadalcanal, served in the artillery. He termed his 1963 memoir, *On Valor's Side*, "a record of a military way of life that is gone" and devoted over half of it to the time he spent training and his experiences prior to landing on Guadalcanal.[27]

As an officer on a battalion staff, Whyte had a better vantage point for viewing the overall campaign than did either Leckie or Gallant. Perhaps because of this, his memoir is far more analytical than either of theirs. Still better positioned were the remaining authors. Samuel Griffith, one of the "Old Breed" of prewar Marines, was a lieutenant colonel who served first as Merritt Edson's executive officer, then succeeded him as commander of the First Raider Battalion. Merrill Twining, a member of Vandegrift's staff, drafted his memoir while recovering from malaria in Australia (though it was not published until a half-century later) and Vandegrift was in overall command of the division. Each produced an interesting book, but each had experiences quite removed from those of a junior officer like Whyte. Griffith did not produce a memoir per se, but during the 1960s both he and Leckie wrote histories containing insights drawn from their months on Guadalcanal.[28]

Among eyewitness writers, perhaps Herbert Christian Merillat had the most in common with Whyte. Both were junior officers who landed on Guadalcanal as lieutenants and left as captains; both were staff officers, Whyte as the Third Battalion's intelligence officer, Merillat as a press officer on the staff of the First Division. Self-styled as "a civilian in uniform, press officer, and in-house historian," Merillat was in a position to have "accumulated a stack of material: a running narrative, notes typed on foolscap, carbon copies of stories written by myself and others on the scene, handwritten entries in a diary, and jottings in a little black looseleaf notebook and on odd bits of paper."[29] He sprinkles extracts from these sources in his narrative, giving it a style unlike any other, but one less personal than Whyte's.

Even more different were the memoirs of E. B. Sledge, an enlisted man in the First Marine Division who fought at Peleliu and Okinawa later in the war. Sledge's *With the Old Breed* is grittier than any of the other memoirs. Whether it is more honest or simply describes more vicious times when troops on both sides had become hardened to human suffering and practiced a more savage creed of kill-or-be-killed is unclear. Sledge did not pass judgment on his fellow Marines, but emphasized that no one who has not been on the line in physical contact with the enemy for an extended period can fully understand the actions of those who have experienced "the violent death, terror, tension, fatigue, and filth that was the infantryman's war."[30] Holly Whyte experienced combat, perhaps of a different type than endured by Sledge—still, both men were First Division Marines and neither ever forgot it.

Notes

1. *The Organization Man* (New York, 1956) sold 225,000 copies in two years.
2. David Riesman, *The Lonely Crowd: A Study of the Changing American Character* (New Haven, 1950); John Kenneth Galbraith, *American Capitalism: The Concept of Countervailing Power* (Boston, 1952) and *The Affluent Society* (New York, 1958); C. Wright Mills, *The Power Elite* (New York, 1956); William Sloan, *The Man in the Gray Flannel Suit* (New York, 1956); and Vance Packard, *The Hidden Persuaders* (New York, 1957). Discussions with my colleague John H. Lenihan helped focus my thoughts on these writers. Eric Goldman, *The Crucial Decade: America, 1945–1955* (New York, 1956) and *The Crucial Decade—and After: America, 1945–1960* (New York, 1960), and John Brooks, *The Great Leap* (New York, 1966), survey American domestic affairs and society in the 1950s.
3. Other authors in this group include C. Wright Mills, *White Collar: The American Middle Classes* (New York, 1951); David Riesman, *Individualism Reconsidered and Other Essays* (New York, 1954); Dwight Macdonald, *Politics Past* (New York, 1957) and *Against the American Grain* (New York, 1962); Paul Goodman, *Growing Up Absurd: Problems of Youth in the Organized System* (New York, 1960); Mary McCarthy, *On the Contrary* (London, 1962); and Daniel Boorstin, *The Image: or What Happened to the American Dream* (New York, 1962). Of these social critics only Mills was almost entirely negative. C. Wright Mills, *The New Men of Power* (New York, 1948), *Character and Social Structure,* with Hans Gerth (New York, 1959), *The Sociological Imagination* (New York, 1959), and *Power, Politics, and People,* a collection of his essays edited by Irving Louis Horowitz (New York, 1963). In a review of *The Organization Man,* Mills wrote that Whyte was addressing "a very old theme—'the bureaucratization of modern society'—and so far as fundamental ideas about it are concerned Mr. Whyte provides nothing new." Mills conceded that Whyte "has fleshed out the well-known bones with up-to-the-minute detail" and applauded Whyte's "account of the organization of the social studies today, with their absurd pretensions," calling it "first rate." Mills, "Crawling to the Top," *New York Times Book Review,* December 9, 1956, 5, 26. For an analysis of the works of these individuals see Richard Pells, *The Liberal Mind in a Conservative Age: American Intellectuals in the 1940s and 1950s* (New York, 1985), 183–88, 232–61, 385.
4. Whyte, *The Organization Man,* 3, 10–15, 182–85.
5. Fortune, *The Exploding Metropolis* (New York, 1958), included an introduction by Whyte and his essays "Are Cities Un-American?" which first appeared in *Fortune* in January 1958, and "Urban Sprawl," which first appeared in *Fortune* in September 1957.
6. "William H. Whyte, 'Organization Man' Author and Urbanologist, Is Dead at 81," *New York Times,* January 13, 1999, B7. Laurance Rockefeller's support of Whyte was personal. Whyte never received significant assistance from any major foundation and had once written an article concluding that independent schol-

ars received very little support from the Rockefeller, Carnegie, and Ford Foundations. "Where the Foundations Fall Down," *Fortune,* November 1955.

7. Whyte first examined the sociology of suburban life in "The Outgoing Life," *Fortune,* June 1953. His books on urban and suburban life include *Securing Open Spaces for Urban America: Conservation Easements* (Washington, D.C., 1959); *Cluster Development* (New York, 1964); *The Last Landscape* (Garden City, N.Y., 1968); *Plan for the City of New York* (editor) (New York, 1969); *The Social Life of Small Urban Spaces* (Washington, D.C., 1980); and *City: Rediscovering the Center* (New York, 1989). See also Jane Jacobs, *The Death and Life of Great American Cities* (New York, 1961).

8. Tulagi and the connected islands of Gavutu-Tanambogo, along with the much larger Florida Island, form the most protected harbor in the southern Solomons, a string of islands stretching southeastward from New Britain, the largest of the Admiralty Islands.

9. Grace P. Hayes, *The History of the Joint Chiefs of Staff in World War II: The War against Japan* (Annapolis, 1982), 136, 141–49; E. B. Potter, *Nimitz* (Annapolis, 1976), 112–14.

10. To conceal the fact that U.S. cryptologists had broken Japan's code, a cover story was concocted saying that a patrol plane had discovered construction of an airfield. Potter, *Nimitz,* 115.

11. Alexander A. Vandegrift, as told to Robert B. Asprey, *Once a Marine* (New York, 1964), 100. Vandegrift and Cates are quoted in Jeter A. Isely and Philip A. Crowl, *The U.S. Marines and Amphibious War* (Princeton, 1951), 115, 121.

12. Vandegrift sent his intelligence officer, Lieutenant Colonel Frank B. Goettge, to Australia to procure maps, aerial photographs, and coastal charts of Guadalcanal and to learn what he could about the island from former residents. After two weeks of hunting, Goettge returned to Wellington with only a few materials. Whyte's view that the Marines never obtained or developed an adequate topographical map of Guadalcanal is correct. When the First Division landed on the island, the best map it had was one pieced together from aerial photographs that covered the area from Aola to Lunga Point and extended only about 2.5 miles inland. There had been significant cloud cover when the high-altitude aerial photographs were taken, so the maps had blank spaces where the clouds had obscured the ground. Goettge brought eight former residents of Guadalcanal to Wellington who would go with the Marines to serve as guides and advisers. Herbert Christian Merillat, *Guadalcanal Remembered* (New York, 1982), 31–32; Richard B. Frank, *Guadalcanal* (New York, 1990), 50.

13. Compare Whyte's brief coverage of the reloading with that accorded it by Merrill B. Twining, *No Bended Knee: The Battle for Guadalcanal: The Memoir of Merrill B. Twining USMC (Ret.)* (Novato, Calif., 1996), 22–36, and Thomas G. Gallant, *On Valor's Side* (Garden City, N.Y., 1963), 179–208. Twining was the First Marine Division's operations officer and Gallant an enlisted man in the division's Fourth Battalion.

14. Fletcher had lost the *Lexington* (CV-2) at Coral Sea and the *Yorktown* (CV-5) at Midway. With only four U.S. carriers remaining in the Pacific, he was reluctant to risk losing more. Indeed, the United States lost two additional carriers and had a third severely damaged before Guadalcanal was secured: *Saratoga* (CV-3) was put out of action for three months by a torpedo from a Japanese submarine on August 13, 1942; *Wasp* (CV-7) was sunk by another Japanese submarine off Guadalcanal on September 15, 1942; and *Hornet* (CV-8) was lost off the Santa Cruz Islands on October 26, 1942. Whyte's assessment of Turner's strategy was a bit harsher than that of Vandegrift, who referred to Turner's "quaint notion of sprinkling little groups of the 7th Marines all over Guadalcanal." Vandegrift, *Once a Marine*, 153. Whyte's view of Fletcher, on the other hand, was shared by virtually all Marines and historians alike. Nimitz later called Fletcher's withdrawal "most unfortunate" because it "left the unloading [transports] and [cargo ships] without air cover." Quoted by Merillat in *Guadalcanal Remembered*, 71. Merillat shared Whyte's assessment of Fletcher; see pp. 67–72 in ibid. For the views of historians, see, for example, Samuel Eliot Morison's official history of the Navy during World War II, which states that "Fletcher's reasons for withdrawal were flimsy" and that "his force could have remained in the area with no more severe consequences than sunburn." Morison, *The Struggle for Guadalcanal* (Boston, 1948), 27–28. See also Isely and Crowl, *U.S. Marines and Amphibious Warfare*, 128–29, and Richard Wheeler, *A Special Valor: The U.S. Marines and the Pacific War* (New York, 1983), 52, who states that "Fletcher's fears for the safety of his carriers got the better of his judgment."

15. Few authors devote more than a page or two to the battle: Vandegrift, *Once a Marine*, 185–86; Merillat, *Guadalcanal Remembered*, 196–97; Eric Hammel, *Guadalcanal: Starvation Island* (New York, 1987), 341–45; Frank, *Guadalcanal*, devotes only two of his 800 pages to the battle (349–50). The Australian coastwatcher Martin Clemens, who served as an adviser to Vandegrift, devotes only four sentences to the attack. Clemens, *Alone on Guadalcanal* (Annapolis, 1998), 266. Whyte mentions Clemens in his memoir, but devotes more space to the exploits of Jacob Charles Vouza, the coastwatcher caught spying by the Japanese, who tortured him and left him for dead. Vouza managed to reach the portion of the Marine front lines held by Whyte's unit. Clemens describes in more graphic detail than Whyte the treatment accorded Vouza, even though Whyte saw Vouza when he first reentered U.S. lines. Ibid., 209–10. Brigadier General Pedro del Valle, commander of Marine artillery units, published an account of the battle in the *Marine Corps Gazette*, February 1944.

16. "Throw Away the Book?" *Marine Corps Gazette*, March 1944, 7–9.

17. "Observation vs. the Jap," *Marine Corps Gazette*, April 1944, 50–52; quote on p. 52.

18. Charles Edmunson, "Why Warriors Fight," *Marine Corps Gazette*, September 1944, 3–10.

19. "Hyakutake Meets the Marines," *Marine Corps Gazette,* July 1945, 2–11, and August 1945, 32–42; quote on p. 3.

20. "Outguessing the Enemy," *Marine Corps Gazette,* November 1945, 15–18, quote on p. 15.

21. "Will the Queen Die?" *Marine Corps Gazette,* January 1946, 10–12; quote on p. 15.

22. "Information into Intelligence," *Marine Corps Gazette,* April 1946, 15–18, and May 1946, 19–23; quotes on pp. 19 and 23.

23. John Hersey, *Into the Valley: A Skirmish of the Marines* (New York, 1943); Richard Tregaskis, *Guadalcanal Diary* (New York and Garden City, N.Y., 1943); Herbert Christian Merillat, *The Island* (Boston, 1943) and *Guadalcanal Remembered;* Robert Leckie, *Helmet for my Pillow* (New York, 1957) and *Challenge for the Pacific: Guadalcanal, the Turning Point of the War* (Garden City, N.Y., 1965); Gallant, *On Valor's Side;* Samuel B. Griffith II, *The Battle for Guadalcanal* (Philadelphia, 1963); Vandegrift, *Once a Marine;* and Twining, *No Bended Knee.* In addition, two aviators, Joe Foss and Thomas G. Miller, Jr., have written memoirs, but Foss did not arrive on Guadalcanal until October 9, and the experiences of pilots were quite different from those of the men on the ground like Whyte. Joe Foss with Walter Simmons, *Joe Foss, Flying Marine: The Story of His Flying Circus* (New York, 1943), and, with Diana Foss, *A Proud American: The Autobiography of Joe Foss* (New York, 1992); Thomas G. Miller, Jr., *The Cactus Air Force* (New York, 1969). Less extensive firsthand accounts of war on Guadalcanal appear in Stanley E. Smith, ed., *The One-Volume History, from Wake to Tsingtao, by the Men Who Fought in the Pacific and by Distinguished Marine Experts, Authors, and Newspaperman* (New York, 1943); and in George McMillan, *The Old Breed: A History of the First Marine Division in World War II* (Washington, D.C., 1949), which was compiled and published by members of the division shortly after the war. Whyte acknowledges consulting the books by Richard B. Frank, Samuel B. Griffith, Alexander A. Vandegrift, Richard Tregaskis, and that of his friend McMillan, whose work he calls "a splendid history of the division," as well as the unpublished memoir of Clifford Cates, when preparing *A Time of War.*

24. Hersey, *Into the Valley.*

25. Tregaskis, *Guadalcanal Diary,* 252–63.

26. Leckie, *Helmet for My Pillow,* 59–139; quoted passage on p. 69.

27. The large amount of space Gallant devoted to the period before Guadalcanal (208 of 364 pages) may reflect the fact that he had letters and notes from that era and that Marines were not allowed to keep diaries or notes while in the war zone. Gallant, *On Valor's Side,* xiii–xiv.

28. Griffith, *The Battle for Guadalcanal,* and Leckie, *Challenge for the Pacific.*

29. Merillat, *Guadalcanal Remembered,* 2.

30. E. B. Sledge, *With the Old Breed* (Novato, Calif., 1981; reprinted, New York, 1990), xvi.

1

Getting Ready

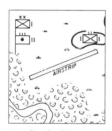 You can draw an outline of my life with maps. Maps showing the hidden paths to the best blueberry patches on Cape Cod. Maps of the downtown streets in my hometown, West Chester, in beautiful Chester County, Pennsylvania. Maps of Noxontown Pond and Silver Lake in Middletown, Delaware, where I went to boarding school. Maps of those terrible rutted roads in the hollows of eastern Kentucky; it was there, straight out of college, that I badgered proprietors of village general stores to buy just one more case of Vicks VapoRub.

Reading maps is easy, once you learn how to do it. I had no idea, though, just how handy this map-reading ability would turn out to be. It paid off in dramatic and unexpected ways for those four and a half months in 1942 that I was on Guadalcanal with McKelvy and the First Marines. We drew maps as we went along, and for much of the time we weren't sure exactly where we were. McKelvy was amazingly consistent in his inability to read the simplest map. He was in one of the Corps' lesser-known proud traditions; he was an original, a character, and an eccentric. He was also bibulous. We had liberated the Japanese sake and beer supply at the outset of the campaign, and McKelvy squirreled a large amount of it away, drinking his way through his private stock the whole time we were there.

I knew about people like Bill McKelvy, too, for I had grown up with some of them. My Uncle Joe Price, a Quaker, sort of—he spoke in "thees" and "thous" anyway—could match McKelvy, the Marine, eccentricity for eccentricity, any day.

The Japanese, we had been told, thought Americans were soft and self-indulgent, and as such would be no match for their tough, experienced, highly disciplined soldiers. I'm sure they didn't all think that way, but we thought they all did, and that's what counts. In the early stages of the World War II, Americans worried about standing up to these fierce little warriors.

But I suspect we were tougher than we, or anyone else, knew, even those among us who had grown up in houses with silver doorknobs, gone away to boarding schools, and attended elite Ivy League colleges such as Princeton.

We had *gangs* when I was a boy in sleepy little West Chester, twenty-five miles west of Philadelphia, with its strong Quaker traditions (no movies, ever, on Sundays). One of my cousins, Alec Hemphill, led the dreaded East End gang. Both sides had guns. They had twenty Daisy and Benjamin air rifles and even a single-shot .22 to our gang's miserable collection of six Daisys and Benjamins. We called ourselves, without much imagination, "the Club," and we thought we were safe in our own tunnel system, essentially a trench covered over with several sheets of galvanized iron. At one point it was seven feet deep, and we had a buried hose through which we could talk with our allies out on the street.

Alec and his henchmen never penetrated the trench, but they did something a lot worse. Alec's younger brother, Dallett, told us day after day that the East End gang was coming after us, but, like the French and the Maginot Line, we thought we were safe in our trench. One day, though, Alec struck, ignoring our trench (just as the Germans ignored the Maginot Line), and he and his East Enders simply tore up the whole area, breaking windows in the house and an arc-light streetlamp at the corner. We were so appalled we fled in mass confusion.

"BANDITS RAID WHYTE HOME," a headline the next day in the *West Chester Daily Local News* said. "PROMINENT ATTORNEY'S SON RING LEADER."

The "prominent attorney's son" was, of course, my cousin Alec Hemphill. Alec was something of a character himself. A year or two after leading the East End gang's attack, he went to my school, St. Andrew's, in Delaware. He was no student, and performed so poorly that his only chance of getting into the University of Pennsylvania was to pass a special course in English composition. I helped in his preparation, and it was an interesting challenge. Out of nowhere he would draw on some hidden literary wellspring, often involving the coining of words never heard before. His favorite phrase was "mistuous innuendo." What did it mean? "It means," he would say, "what I mean it to mean." It's hard to stay mad at someone who writes, and thinks, like that. To the amazement of his instructors, his friends, and myself, Alec passed the special course. His English teacher at St. Andrew's, scenting a scandal, accused me of prepping Alec too well. But, in his own stubborn way, Alec loved literature, and he passed on his own merits. "Mistuous innuendo" indeed. A few months later, he was elected president of his freshman class at Penn. Long after that, he was elected, and reelected again and again, as Philadelphia's city controller.

All of us—East Enders included—enjoyed growing up in West Chester. It's the seat of Chester County, with its beautiful Brandywine Valley. We roamed everywhere, town and country, and it was so easy to do. The country began exactly where the town ended. It was laid out in a row-house pattern created by a man named Cumming, one of William Penn's surveyors. The neighborhoods are continuous and nicely dovetailed. As a consequence, West Chester is a very walkable town. You can walk from the edge of town to the center in fifteen minutes or less. That doesn't mean most West Chester people walk very much. They don't. But they could if they wanted to.

When I was a boy, I spent much of my time in and around my Grandmother Whyte's house; it had been the summer home of her father, Joshua Hartshorne, a wealthy Baltimore merchant. He was in trade, the rest of the family muttered, and so he was never held in very high regard. But he must have been a sport: the doorknobs really were silver. After she died, we used the place as a sort of ghost house.

The Brandywine Valley wasn't far away, and all we had to do was climb on our bicycles and pedal to get there. It was in this valley, of course, that George Washington and his Continental army suffered one of their most frustrating defeats. There were several crossing points—places where the creek could be forded—but the local farmers, most of them Quakers with Tory sympathies, failed to alert the rebel general which of them General Howe's soldiers were preparing to cross. Washington, blinded by lack of proper intelligence, sought at one point to join his own troops, but he had lost track of exactly where they were. In any event, the British forded the creek and put the rebels to rout after a short, but spirited, action. It was an early lesson in the importance of combat intelligence—and good maps.

My Grandfather Price, a surgeon, married a devout Quaker and bought a place called "Valley Farms" in the rolling hills of Chester Valley, where they proceeded to rear nine children. It was a good family, as families go. The girls were the belles of the valley, and the boys were worthwhile except Uncle Joe. The way I remember him, he was short and squat, with a large, straight nose, intense gray eyes, and a magnificent black, bristling moustache. Immensely powerful—I think he was the strongest man I have ever known—he preferred the company of local rowdies and roughnecks to the sociable set surrounding the rest of his family. When he did show up at the parties at the farm, he was almost always drunk—and looking for a fight.

College, everyone thought, would have a softening influence. But after several hectic weeks at the University of Pennsylvania, Joe was back home. It was then that Grandfather deemed it was time to take stern measures; he told Joe that from now on he was a farmhand. To everyone's surprise, he turned out to be a good one. But being a farmhand wasn't enough for Uncle Joe. To make a little petty cash, he developed a troubling habit—selling off the farm's livestock. The straw hit the fan when it was discovered that he had secretly taken out a mortgage on his parents' farm. The family woke up one morning in 1916 to discover that Grandfather's best carriage and the horses that went with it were missing. So, of course, was Uncle Joe.

As far as we knew, Uncle Joe drifted from job to job before joining the Navy in World War I. He showed up after the war at his mother's summer home on Cape Cod. Joe's mother, my Grandmother Price, was a formidable figure. Her house was next to a pond at Wellfleet that once belonged to a sea captain named Holcombe. We spent our summers there, and it was Grandmother who first started me thinking about maps. There was a sandy slope on the far side of the pond that, in season, was overrun with wild blueberries and blackberries. She told me to pick them, and her order was my command. I became something of an expert, both on berries and on the hidden paths that led to them. I learned then to make maps. The maps were crude—they had to be—but they were the only maps we had.

And what berries they were. Sweet juicy ones. We had them with syrup and we had them on cereal. Commercial berries were never half so good.

It was at Wellfleet that I first got to know Uncle Joe. By then he was a local institution, an amazing character serving as a fine introduction to those eccentrics who make the United States Marine Corps so special. Uncle Joe would have been a fine addition to the Corps' roster of eccentrics.

I think he really was one of the nicest things about our summers in Wellfleet, even if he did have a terrible temper and even though his stories didn't always ring true. He was the family's black sheep.

After Grandmother's old house (by now, Grandfather was dead) was turned into an inn called Holiday House, Uncle Joe would hold court with the guests and tell stories. His favorite was about the great, though indecisive, battle between the British and German grand fleets at Jutland in World War I. Uncle Joe, a young ensign in the U.S. Navy, was there. At least he said he was. Not only was he there, he was actually on the same bridge with the British admiral, David Beatty. He was there when Beatty, watching his vulnerable battle cruisers burst into flame and sink, turned to his flag captain to say, "Something seems to be wrong with our bloody ships today." Uncle Joe swore he had seen it all, and he remembered especially a young British officer with red hair. Right there on the bridge. A telling detail, lending verisimilitude to all the rest of his story. Joe never elaborated any further. He wound up the story with a flourish of his hand, and suddenly departed. It was always a wonderful performance.

Uncle Joe was more than just a storyteller; he tended to collect things, often other people's things. Some folks around Wellfleet would joke they didn't dare to go away on weekends for fear Uncle Joe would burgle their houses. And, in fact, he did have a critical eye for fine old artifacts, including large portions of front porches and other considerable architectural details.

His methodology was simple. "Holly," he would say, meaning me (like my father before me, my nickname is a shortened version of our middle name, Hollingsworth), "would thee and thy little friends like to help thy Uncle Joe clean up the house?" The little friends, as often as not, were the Hemphill boys, Alec, of East Ender fame, and his brother, Dallett. The house to be cleaned up inevitably belonged to someone else.

One summer, Uncle Joe magically found enough money to buy himself a thirty-five-foot auxiliary sailboat named *Ethel B*. From that day on most of his time was spent caulking and painting his treasure, and sometimes even sailing it. By a variety of subtle ruses we were inveigled into such tasks as bailing out the oily water or swabbing the deck. We never suspected he might have had a self-serving motive in permitting us to help out in this way. To our envious friends, we explained that the *Ethel B.* was a Coast Guard cutter engaged in running down the bootleggers that swarmed the shores of Cape Cod during these Prohibition years, and that we were part of the crew. Naturally enough, with all this reflected glory, our position among the young people in Wellfleet was impregnable.

Uncle Joe had also bought a new car to go along with his sailboat. This, of course, was puzzling, for Uncle Joe had no obvious source of income. It was not until one memorable August night that the truth finally dawned.

Grandmother had decided to go to Hyannis for a couple of days to visit some friends. My friend Norbert was visiting me, and this seemed to open up the opportunity we had been waiting for—to spend a night on the North Shore of the Cape, a place so lonely everyone knew it was where the bootleggers rendezvoused. The North Shore near Wellfleet was a fascinating place, barren and desolate with a majesty of its own. The beach is about a hundred yards deep, coming to an end at the huge bluffs. The surf is so heavy that no one swims there. Every half mile or so the battered skeleton of an old schooner lies half buried under the sand, mute witness to the Cape's past.

Barren and desolate it may have been, but it was paradise for us. We alternated between sliding down the sand dunes and riding the surf on top of an empty oil barrel. We settled on the wreck of an old schooner as the place we would spend the night, started a fire, and cooked supper. Later, we walked to the top of the bluff and surveyed our desolate domain. Five miles away we could make out the lights of Wellfleet. Occasionally we could see the lights of a coastal steamer out at sea. It was the kind of night that turns teenage boys into mature philosophers, and so Norbert and I talked at some length about what was out there beyond the stars.

We were just settling down—a little scared already—when the unmistakable sound of groaning oarlocks alerted us to the fact that a dory was being beached nearby. Bootleggers! Now we were really scared. We all knew that bootleggers didn't welcome witnesses. We cleared out of the old hull and scrambled up the dunes, where we could see a light off in the distance. It blinked on and off, convincing us it was one bootlegger signaling to another. A truck pulled up on the beach, and we saw three men unloading what appeared to be cases of whiskey from the boat and putting them in the back of the truck. One of the men looked suspiciously like Uncle Joe. With barely enough light to see, we raced across the moors to Grandmother's house and the welcome sounds of Grandmother's friend, Mrs. Dalmas, playing the piano.

Two weeks later, the season over, we left for home. I wasn't sure how to handle our discovery that Uncle Joe was a bootlegger—that, of course, was the source of his mysterious income—but in the end I convinced myself that what he was doing wasn't such a bad thing after all. Bootleggers were adventurers, and so were we. Uncle Joe remained my friend.

In the fall of 1931, to everyone's surprise and consternation, Uncle Joe got married. His wife, Eulalia, as far as we could tell, had been a salesperson—sales girl then—in a dry goods store in Pittsburgh. They arrived the next summer in Wellfleet in what Uncle Joe called a "house car"—he had built it himself out of the remains of an old bus and several automobiles. The house car was such an impressive sight that the *National Geographic,* swearing it was an authentic piece of motor transportation history, ran a picture of it.

Grandmother Price, taking pity on the newlyweds, told Uncle Joe that he and Eulalia could live at Holiday House and take in boarders. Grandmother died soon after making that decision, and in her will she provided that Uncle Joe could use Holiday House for the rest of his life, although members of the family could come and visit if they wished.

Eulalia had a gypsy look to her—she would roam the inn's corridors at night in her long, swooping robes—and she drew to the inn an interesting collection of New York writers and German psychiatrists. Her Sunday-night suppers were famous from one end of the Cape to the other. She loved practical jokes. One of them was a sign above a guest-room toilet that read, "Please don't throw cigarette butts into the toilet. It makes them soggy and hard to light."

Years later, after most of the family had given up their Cape summers, Uncle Joe, by all accounts, began to move from eccentricity into a somewhat dangerous form of dementia. It was whispered that he had even beaten up Eulalia once or twice—knowing Eulalia, we figured this was no mean feat. It got to the point where Eulalia had the Commonwealth of Massachusetts declare him to be, in effect, a mental case. He disappeared after that, and we all thought he was dead. One summer, though, he showed up again, telling everyone he was piloting airplanes and studying celestial navigation. That was the last we knew of Uncle Joe.

I went away to St. Andrew's School—it was brand new, with no trees and the grass just beginning to take hold—when I was fourteen, in eighth grade. It was founded as an Episcopal Church academy by members of the du Pont family, and it exalted what educators called "muscular Christianity," based on English boarding-school traditions. We worked in the kitchen and scrubbed the floors and made our own beds. As eighth and ninth graders, we lived in great, drafty dormitories that would make a Marine Corps drill instructor flinch. But we learned things, especially how to write, thanks largely to a brilliant English teacher named Bill Cameron. (The school is all grown up now, rich with tradition and tall trees. A movie, *Dead Poets Society,* was even filmed on campus, because the school looked so much like a proper New England boarding school.)

By the time we were sixth formers, or twelfth graders, we were attending debutante dances in the ballroom at the Barclay Hotel in Philadelphia and making plans to go to college. My choice was Princeton, and by the time I was finished it was June of 1939 and the war clouds were already moving across Europe. We didn't think much about that. We worried about our careers. We talked about individualism a lot, but we didn't practice it much. My friends were joining big corporations, early examples of *The Organization Man* at work. I moved into the management-training program of the Vick Chemical Company.

It was a school, really—the Vick School of Applied Merchandising—and it wasn't all that different, in concept, from the Marines' Officers Candidate School at Quantico, Virginia. "The Vick curriculum was . . . survival of the fittest," I wrote in *The Organization Man.* "The Vick school . . . was frankly based on the principle of elimination. It wouldn't make any difference how wonderful all of us would be, of the 38 of us who [began the program], the rules of the game dictated that only six or seven of us would be asked to stay with Vick."

After a touch of schooling in New York, we were sent out into the field to see if the blood of the true rapacious salesman ran through the veins of any of us. I was sent to the hill country of eastern Kentucky with a car (the clutch system kept breaking down), a full supply of signs, a ladder, a stock of samples, and an order pad.

The roads were what I remember most. "Half of the time," I wrote my father in November of 1939, "they're dry stream beds—their maps fail to advise that a little rain changes them back to their original state." That's a nice point. We would encounter exactly the same phenomenon on

Guadalcanal. "I ford at least three streams a day," I wrote in 1939, "and with some apprehension as the water gets deeper. You just have to be optimistic. This Thursday I ran into the worst one yet—40 miles of driving (all in first or second gear) along cliffs, over logs, rocky streams, etc. Finally, just at 6 p.m. as I was starting on the 20-mile trek back to (my hotel) in Greenup the car sputtered and dismally died. After a bad day, no sales etc., a lunch of 'Vienee' sausage and soda crackers, this was about the last straw. Very fortunately a farmer passed by in his truck, and hauled me all 20 miles into Greenup. The mechanic found that the carburetor had shaken loose from the feed lines, the ignition wires had become disconnected, the choke had become stuck, the fan belt loosened, the generator jogged out of place. I was amazed the whole car hadn't fallen apart."

On a typical day, I would get up at 6:00 or 6:30 a.m. in some bleak boardinghouse or run-down hotel and after a greasy breakfast set off to staple Vicks signs on barns and telephone poles. At about 8:00 I would make my first visit to one of the local general stores, where we were supposed to talk the proprietor into purchasing a year's supply of Vicks products, all at once. Having pulled that off, we would give a vivid display of one of the many Vicks products. "Tilt your head back, Mr. Jones," we would say to the dealer. And then we would quickly shoot a whopping dropper-full of Vatronol up his nose.

I enjoyed the challenge of making sales to these tough old country-store patriarchs. "Most of them are friendly, but some of them are mean as the devil," I wrote my father. "They're really scared to death of salesmen, afraid we'll 'put something over' on them. They've seen the sun rise the same way for 60 years, their wife has worn the same dress for 60 years, their store hasn't changed, and so they see no reason why a 'new-fangled' nose drop should sell, since they didn't sell 60 years ago."

I was a miserable salesman at first. I lied to myself about why I was doing so badly. "The local brick plant is shut down here," I wrote in my diary, "and nobody's buying anything." A wise old salesman came to see how I was doing. He got straightaway to the core of my problem. "Whyte," he said, "you are never going to sell a damn thing until you realize that the man on the other side of the counter is your enemy." That did it. In no time I was selling everything in sight and taking immense pleasure in screwing ugly metal signs advertising Vicks products into the dealers' beloved old oak paneling. My first week I had averaged 48 percent in sales to calls; by the time I caught on, I was averaging 74 percent.

"It was truly an experience," I wrote in *The Organization Man,* "and if we shudder to recall the things we did, we must admit that as a cram course in reality it was extraordinarily efficient."

I don't suppose the Japanese strategists ever heard about either Uncle Joe or the Vick School of Applied Merchandising. It might have changed their minds about just how naive and soft we really were.

2

Joining Up

 "Whyte, William Hollingsworth Third," the drill instructor roared at our first roll call at the Officers Candidate School in Quantico, Virginia, on October 28, 1941. "Jesus," he added, his voice dripping with sarcasm, "what a moniker."

It was my first Marine Corps lesson: Keep it simple. From then on I was Whyte, William H., Jr.

Why did I join the Marine Corps? More to the point, why did I join when there was no compulsion to sign up? We were still at peace, though my father and I, both interventionists, believed we would—and should— soon be at war. The Marine Corps was accepting only volunteers, and it took downright pleasure in promising the toughest kind of training.

Ego was involved, I suppose. In my way of thinking, the Marine Corps was the best, and I wanted to be a part of it. If you're going to go, why not go with the one truly elite outfit in the U.S. armed services?

So here I was, a candidate for second lieutenant, and my sarcastic drill instructor—I remember his name was Sergeant Catalano—didn't seem at all sure that I was doing the Marine Corps much of a favor.

The United States Marines are a kind of religion, and Quantico is their temple. It is a place for ritual, and there's no room for monkey business.

Sergeants run the show, and to watch them at work is to be impressed by their skills at putting us, lowly beginners, down, and then in building us up, so that we can say we are Marines.

Sergeant Catalano was a master of the double take, seemingly forever astonished by our witless responses to his questions.

At the time I joined up, the entire Marine Corps consisted of about 65,000 officers and men; by the time the war ended, the Marines numbered 37,664 officers and 485,113 men, six entire divisions, and four air wings.

Whatever their size, big or small, the Marines tend to play a special role in American life. Almost from the beginning, what so often kept the Marines in the public eye was the fact that so many of their officers and enlisted men seemed to be larger than life. Take, for example, Gunnery Sergeant Daniel J. "Fighting Dan" Daly, who won *two* Medals of Honor, the first in the Boxer Rebellion in China, the second in Haiti. He capped this off by winning a Navy Cross and an Army Distinguished Service Cross at the Marines' great victory over the Germans at Belleau Wood in World War I.

It was Daly, at forty-four years of age, who led his machine-gun company across an open wheat field in an action observed by Floyd Gibbons, war correspondent for the *Chicago Tribune*. "This old sergeant," Gibbons wrote in a famous dispatch, "was a Marine veteran. His cheeks were bronzed with the wind and sun of the seven seas. The service bar across his chest showed he had fought in the Philippines, in Santo Domingo, at the walls of Pekin, and in the streets of Vera Cruz.

"As the minute for the advance arrived, he arose from the trees first and jumped out onto the exposed edge of that field that ran with lead, across which his men were to charge. Then he turned to give the charge order to the men of his platoon—his mates—the men he loved. 'Come on, you sons-o'bitches! Do you want to live forever?'"

Sergeant Catalano loved to quote another great line, attributing it to Captain Williams at the bloody World War I battle of Chateau-Thierry in June of 1918. When asked if he and his Marines were prepared to retreat in the face of crushing German opposition, he replied: "Retreat hell! We just got here." Marine historians aren't sure who uttered the line, but someone said it, and it became part of the Marine Corps' cherished folklore.

Best known of all these pre–World War II Marines was Smedley ("Old Gimlet Eye") Darlington Butler, a rambunctious, teetotaling Quaker (of sorts, anyway) from my hometown, West Chester.

Butler fought in most of these "banana wars" and always remained convinced that serving as colonial infantry was the main mission of the Marine Corps. In one of them, in Nicaragua in 1912, he served side by side with William N. ("Wild Bill") McKelvy, father of the man who would lead my battalion on Guadalcanal. The two of them, both majors, led their Marines against a well-defended hilltop outside Masaya, in the western part of the country, and routed the rebel commander, Zeledon, and the thousand men serving under him in a sharp little action that brought the insurrection to an end.

In the years following World War I, as the colonial era and the wars that went with it began winding down, some farsighted Marines (Butler not among them) concluded they needed to find a mission for the Corps that would stave off the constant efforts by a jealous Army to whittle the Marines down to size.

Readiness was an obvious concept. After all, the Marines had bulldozed their way into World War I, against Army opposition, as the proud unit that was "First to Fight." The problem was, the Marines fought just like soldiers (they would do so again, with tragic consequences, in Vietnam). What the Marines needed, these farsighted officers agreed, was a special role. They needed to be ready to fight in ways the Army couldn't, or wouldn't.

The answer was supplied in large part by an amazing and enigmatic figure, Earl H. "Pete" Ellis, who decided as early as 1915 that the United States one day would go to war against Japan. In 1921, Ellis, then a Marine lieutenant colonel, predicted in a top-secret paper called "Advanced Base Operations in Micronesia" that Japan would attack first and that the United States would be forced to strike back by capturing a number of advanced bases in the Pacific Ocean theater. "It will be necessary for us to project our fleet and landing forces across the Pacific and wage war in Japanese waters," he said. "To effect this requires that we have sufficient bases to support the fleet, both during the projection and afterward."

He said the Marines would need to think about special equipment—amphibious landing craft, for example. In his history of the Marine Corps, *Soldiers of the Sea,* Robert D. Heinl points out that Ellis predicted that it would require two reinforced regiments to capture Eniwetok, in the Marshall Islands, one of the advanced bases he said the United States would need in a war with Japan. In 1944, the United States captured Eniwetok—with two reinforced regiments.

Ellis, fluent in Japanese, took a leave of absence from the Marines in 1922 and began poking his way around the Pacific, visiting Japanese-held islands. He said he was a commercial traveler, but of course he was a spy. He eventually made his way to the Palaus, scene of terrible fighting on little Peleliu Island in the fall of 1944. He stayed on an island called Koror, living with a native woman. Ellis was an alcoholic, with a long history of drying-out episodes in hospitals. He was drinking heavily on Koror, and it may have killed him. The Japanese say that's what happened. American researchers suggest he was seized as a spy by Japanese police, and executed. His fate remains a mystery.

But his legacy lived on as the Marines' precious, Corps-saving new fighting concept—amphibious warfare. With the enthusiastic support of the commandant, Major General John A. Lejeune, Ellis's thirty-thousand-word paper eventually became the celebrated Fleet Training Publication No. 167, *Landing Operations Doctrine, U.S. Navy,* published in 1938 and copied word for word by the Army as its Field Manual 31-5. In either version, it was the basis for every Allied amphibious operation in World War II.

Marine Corps historian J. Robert Moskin notes that the manual was extraordinary for the detail it contained. It covered almost everything—from "the nature of the landing force, the coordination of close-air support, the allocation of command responsibilities, ship-to-shore movements . . . logistics, the combat-loading of transports, the use of landing craft."

It flew in the face of conventional wisdom—that troops could not be landed from the sea against well-entrenched troops onshore. That, the critics of amphibious warfare said, was the lesson of the great British disaster against the well-entrenched Turks at Gallipoli in World War I.

But these Marine thinkers had studied Gallipoli in the Dardanelles and concluded that the operation should have been a success. Initially, the Marines found, the British landing had gone very well. But then, as the Turks grew more aggressive, the British and their Australian allies began to suffer doubts, though Winston Churchill, who thought the idea up in the first place, remained optimistic until the end. The loss of the Dardanelles was as much a psychological defeat as it was anything else.

When I arrived at Quantico to become a candidate for second lieutenant in the Marine Corps, I had never heard of Pete Ellis or Fleet Training Publication 167. That changed quickly, for by the time we got our gold bars all of us had been required to study 167. I remember memorizing huge chunks of it.

My father, Holly Whyte, Sr., saved many of the letters I wrote to him and Margaret, my stepmother, from the time I joined the Marines. Here's one of my reports from Quantico:

> The night problems are something—tramping and scrambling around brush and soaked to the skin. Get in about 10:30 p.m., clean equipment, bed at 11 p.m. Up at 5:40 a.m. As a result when we all had our physical exams a lot of us had heart flutters never noticed before. I'm scared stiff I may not pass. But if I do, I get my commission on the 31st [of January 1942, when the war was barely a month old]. Find out tomorrow or Thursday about the exam.
>
> We have landing operations tomorrow and the temperature of the water will be on the cool side. Go up the coast to Maryland [Solomons Island, Maryland, in curious fact] to make the landing, then have a "problem" without a change of clothes. The sergeants say "Tutten ye' up!" but they wish they could get off [from this duty].
>
> Many, many thanks for the $15. It really helps.
>
> P.S. I MADE IT. Just got the news. Physical exam OK.

The training was tough, pretty much the standard indoctrination boots received at Parris Island and San Diego. Much of it had to do with physical things—rifles to be field-stripped, jungle gyms to climb, mock grenades to be hurled—but the core of Marine training is in matters of the spirit, and Marines never forget that.

The Corps is sparing of honors. The highest honor recruits can aspire to is the uniform—a bilious green, I always thought—and, of course, the globe-and-anchor badge that goes with it.

It is as an elite force that the Marine Corps must be judged. It is no bad thing that recruits are indoctrinated. It is the top of the hill they are taught to take, and they know it. So I have never thought we should begrudge Marines their eccentricities. On a cost/benefit ration, the Marines have always been a great bargain for the American taxpayer.

More than the Army or the Navy, the smaller Marine Corps sees itself as a brotherhood. Alexander Archer Vandegrift, the major general who commanded the Marines on Guadalcanal, recalls in his autobiography that just before the war started he and two or three of his closest colleagues could honestly say that between them they knew every officer in the Corps. It really was a family.

Victor H. "Brute" Krulak, a Marine general—and, more family, father of the Marine commandant in 1997—calls it a "mystical" brotherhood.

It's spelled out in an unusual document, the 1921 Marine Corps manual, written by General Lejeune and still applicable today. "The [first] World War," Lejeune wrote, "wrought a great change in relations between officers and enlisted men in the military services. A spirit of comradeship and brotherhood in arms came into being in the training camps and on the battlefields. This spirit is too fine a thing to be allowed to die."

So it is that new recruits are told that "a Marine believes in his God, in his country, in his Corps, in his buddies, and in himself." Brute Krulak had those words painted on signs at the entrance to the San Diego boot camp when he commanded it.

These notions may seem quaint and old-fashioned to baby boomer and Generation X Americans today. That may explain why the separation between the Marines' world and the civilians' world is wider than ever.

The Marines' answer to that is a shrug of the shoulders. They mean to get on with their business.

And their business for all these years has been amphibious warfare. They began practicing landings as early as the 1920s, and one of the problems that plagued them from the start was finding a suitable boat to get them and their equipment from their transports to the shore. Early on, the Marines tried barges or lighters towed to shore by other, motorized boats, but that wasn't practicable. Next was the "Beetle Boat," with a steel canopy that would have prevented Marines from making an evacuation should something go wrong. Brute Krulak, who was involved in these disastrous experiments, wrote that the Beetle Boat "had no surf capability at all, was extremely hard to control, and had no provision whatever for carrying motor vehicles."

Pete Ellis had come up with the theory. Now, another amazing figure emerged to give the Marines, and soon the Army, the boat they needed to storm beaches from Guadalcanal to Normandy. His name was Andrew Jackson Higgins, and he built boats. Brute Krulak played a role too. As an observer of Japanese landings at the mouth of the Yangtze River in 1937, he had seen, and photographed, Japanese landing craft, with their bow ramps, that rode right up on the beaches so that heavy vehicles could be unloaded.

When Higgins finally was asked to design such a landing craft for the

Marines, he converted a forty-five-foot steel lighter he had built for the government of Colombia into a bow-ramp landing craft capable of carrying an eighteen-ton tank. He built this boat in sixty-one hours. The Marines, Brute Krulak said, "were ecstatic."

But not the Navy's Bureau of Ships. They stuck by their own design, until Harry Truman, then a U.S. senator, intervened, and said get on with Higgins's boat. The navy initially ordered two hundred of them—the famous LCVPs (Landing Craft, Vehicle and Personnel). Marine General Holland M. ("Howlin' Mad") Smith would say later that the Higgins boat "contributed more to our common victory than any other single piece of equipment used in the war." An exaggeration, surely, but not by much.

Andrew Jackson Higgins was a great man.

That was the boat we were practicing with in those landings at Maryland's Solomons Island. That was the boat that would take us ashore at Guadalcanal. But we were just second lieutenants, worried about getting along with the first platoon of Marines we had ever commanded, and we didn't think much about what a beautiful thing it was.

From 1934 to 1941, the Marines' basic fighting strength was represented by two brigades, the First, on the East Coast, "the Raggedy-Ass Marines," and the Second, on the West Coast near the place where they made movies, "the Hollywood Marines." With our gold bars, we were ordered to New River, North Carolina, to the training camp of what had been the First Brigade and what would now become the First Marine Division, the "Old Breed," the first full division ever mustered in Marine Corps history. And we were all scared to death.

New River was no paradise. It had been cut out of swamps, and the only living accommodations were in tents. "As usual," my friend the Marine war correspondent George McMillan wrote in his splendid campaign history of the division, "there was gum-beating and enamel chipping. The men complained that conditions at New River were not happenstance. 'This is the way they want things,' one salt explained. 'You don't make a good fightin' man if you're in love with everybody.' You gotta be mad, so sore at everything you'd slug your best buddy at the drop of a p....cutter.'" (McMillan is talking, delicately, about a cap the Marines called a pisscutter.)

We knew we—ninety-day wonders from officers school—were to be given platoons, platoons composed to a great degree of old-timers, men who had fought in Nicaragua and Haiti. You can understand that we, civilians only a few months earlier, were apprehensive of the reception that awaited us.

It was no wonder. These Marines we were about to command were extraordinary. Maybe no one has described them better than Samuel B. Griffith II, who would take part in the Guadalcanal campaign.

> They were a motley bunch. Hundreds were young recruits only recently out of boot training at Parris Island. Others were older; first sergeants yanked off "planks" in Navy yards, sergeants from recruiting duty, gunnery sergeants who had fought in France, perennial privates with disciplinary records a yard long. These were the professionals, the "Old Breed" of United States Marines. Many had fought "Cacos" in Haiti, "bandidos" in Nicaragua, and French, English, Italian, and American sailors in every bar in Shanghai, Manila, Tsingtao, Tientsin, and Peking.
>
> They were inveterate gamblers and accomplished scroungers, who drank hair tonic in preference to post-exchange beer ("horse piss"), cursed with wonderful fluency, and never went to chapel ("the God box") unless forced to. Many dipped snuff, smoked rank cigars or chewed tobacco (cigarettes were for women and children). . . . They knew their weapons and they knew their tactics. They knew they were tough and they knew they were good. There were enough of them to leaven the Division and to impart to the thousands of younger men a share of the unique spirit which they animated and the skills they possessed.

The man who would lead my battalion on Guadalcanal, Lieutenant Colonel McKelvy, was just this kind of "Old Breed" Marine. I met him for the first time at New River. He was a well-built man of middling height, square-jawed, with a great booming voice. The odd thing about him was that, from the time I first met him, he seemed to be under some kind of extraordinary tension. He was always . . . apprehensive. Apprehensive, I was to learn, about higher authority (and higher authority was sometimes apprehensive about him).

He was born in Brooklyn, New York, on January 24, 1900, the son of a Marine Corps officer. He was graduated from the U.S. Naval Academy at Annapolis in June of 1921 and began a series of duty tours that marked the life of a professional, "peacetime" Marine. He served with Marine detachments at several naval yards before shipping out to Santo Domingo with the Second Brigade in 1923. He served later with the Sixth and Twelfth Marines in Tientsin, China, and made his way to Nicaragua in 1928.

By 1937 he was a company commander and was sent to study in the Senior Course at the Marine Schools at Quantico. He joined the First Marine Division at Quantico in June of 1941, and was already commanding the Third Battalion, First Marines, when I arrived at New River smack out of Officers Candidate School. I've been thinking about him ever since.

After the war, when I had just begun working at *Fortune* magazine, I gave a commencement address at my old boarding school, St. Andrew's, in Middletown, Delaware. I tried to make the point to the young boys listening to me that sometimes it pays to stick your neck out, instead of just following the mob. It does sound a little like the theme I returned to not so much later in *The Organization Man*.

At any rate, I said that one of us from my Officers Candidate School class did stick his neck out. His name was Harold Kirby Taylor, twenty-four years old when he was commissioned.

Taylor, I told these school kids, was a model, a sterling character. He'd had a fine record in school in Cleveland Heights, Ohio. He was an exceptional athlete. But the period of his life he was proudest of was the time he spent in the Boy Scouts. This naturally provoked derision from us, and I said in my speech that we couldn't begin to count the nicknames we coined on the strength of his idealization of the Boy Scouts of America. Worse than this, he lectured us incessantly on our somewhat lackadaisical attitude toward the military profession. While we played bridge, he studied, and often as we were going to sleep we could hear the click of his rifle as he practiced the manual of arms in the shower room. We liked him, I said, but he was always good for a laugh.

That first day we took over our new platoons, we suffered. The old gunnery sergeants didn't even try to conceal their amusement, and the men smiled knowingly as we marched them into ditches. We forgot all the commands we had been taught and generally made fools of ourselves. But slowly, day by day, we grew more confident, more capable, but still hesitant to exercise authority. We wanted to be liked, so we pretended not to notice when the men didn't salute us. We dismissed the men in our platoons as early in the afternoon as we could. We couldn't have been more ingratiating.

But not Taylor. His men marched and trained from dawn to dusk and frequently half the night. Anyone who failed to salute him got extra duty.

And while he took care to make sure his men were properly fed and their equipment was as good as anyone else's, he also made sure his men didn't have time to visit the honky-tonks surrounding our camp.

We were amused by all of this. We were sure that this spit and polish, this strict discipline, was obsolete. Our policy was to talk things over with the men and not worry if their close-order drill was a little sloppy. We were going to have one great big happy family! The sad truth is, we were afraid to exercise leadership, afraid we might be rejected.

We thought Taylor's men would be the first to reject their platoon commander when we faced the enemy. What we didn't appreciate was the obvious fact that his men loved him. They called him "Ramrod," and the nickname stuck. They would go anywhere with him, and my own men on Guadalcanal were quick to volunteer to join him on patrol.

Ramrod Taylor was one hell of a Marine. He died a hero on Guadalcanal, winning the Navy Cross posthumously (we'll pick up his story later). He is buried in Grave 1483, Section 12, Arlington National Cemetery, just across the river from the nation's capital.

3

Shipping Out

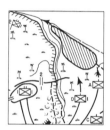 Hundreds of thousands of us wrote dramatic letters home just like this one:

Dear Dad and Margaret:

A note to let you know I won't be home next weekend, nor, I am afraid, any weekend for a good long time. Can't tell you much more save that you won't be getting any letters from me for a long time as the only thing I can send is a standard form card with my unit number and a post office box. That will be sent to you by the Navy after we've sailed. Please be sure and write.

The men are in great spirits tonight, perhaps because they've been consuming copious amounts of beer for several hours. The songs are getting randier and randier with every beer.

Certainly nice to see you last weekend and am sorry won't have any more until after Hitler has folded. Can't tell you much more for reasons you can well understand. Be sure and write.

Love, Holly

Hitler, of course, wasn't so much our particular problem. We were the Marines, and our war was in the Pacific against the Japanese. We were heading for Wellington, New Zealand, where we expected to settle down for six months of intensive training before mounting our first attack against the enemy.

We would be, grandly, the Landing Force of the South Pacific Amphibious Force. But we were hardly in anything approaching fighting trim. One of our regiments, the Seventh Marines, had been taken away from us and shipped out to defend Samoa, and we wouldn't see these fine troops again for months.

Then there was the problem with the new Raider battalions. The Marines now had two of them (the First, commanded by Merritt Edson, and the Second, commanded by Evans Carlson). To General Vandegrift's chagrin, Edson showed up to pick out the best men we had to form the nucleus of his new Raider battalion. Vandegrift said, sensibly, that he saw no point in forming elite units from units that already were elite. But President Roosevelt and Navy Secretary Frank Knox had become enamored of the British commando units and wanted some of their own. If that wasn't bad enough, grumbled Vandegrift, the Marines were also forced to form "parachutist battalions, beachjumpers, glider units, barrage balloon units and war-dog platoons."

Carlson was one of those classic Marine characters. He had developed his own theories of warfare by traveling with and observing the tactics of the Communist Chinese Eighth Route Army. He picked up the phrase "Gung ho!" from the Chinese and made it a part of the Marines' language. Carlson came late in the struggle for Guadalcanal and promptly set off in pursuit of a Japanese regiment in his own private thirty-day campaign. We sometimes thought of him as a latter-day Jeb Stuart, disappearing when Robert E. Lee needed him most.

We admired Edson's Raider battalion. It took part in the key battle for a ridge that would be known afterwards as "Edson's Ridge," and he and his men were much more traditional in their outlook.

What we really needed were infantry regiments. The Marines use confusing nomenclature. They call their regiments "Marines." We were, for example, the First Marines, one of three infantry regiments in the First Marine Division. Each rifle regiment contained three rifle battalions. Each rifle battalion contained three rifle companies. The division also contained an artillery regiment—ours was the Eleventh Marines—and on Guadalcanal the Eleventh Marines fired their 75mm pack howitzers with devastating effect. With everyone included, a Marine division early in World War II numbered about 19,500 men.

Fleet Training Publication No. 167 had outlined procedures for combat-loading of transport ships, so that the stuff we needed first came out first. But in shoving off—some of us from Norfolk, the rest of us from San Francisco—we hadn't had the time for that.

Now that we were back together again in New Zealand, we had to do it right. That meant all the supplies had to be unloaded and then loaded the right way. Right away we bumped into an unexpected problem. New Zealand—now smack in the path of the Japanese juggernaut—was run by a socialist party, and the strongest advocates of socialist theory worked on the docks as longshoremen.

General Vandegrift was apoplectic. "Just what in hell is wrong?" he demanded when he first arrived in Wellington's beautiful harbor. "They work differently from us," he was told by Merrill Twining, a key aide who had been sent ahead to arrange our stay in New Zealand. Twining, by then a colonel, would be my co-lecturer on the meaning of the Guadalcanal campaign when the fighting was over and we were both back at Quantico. But here he was, just a major, facing a very angry general. "They stop for morning tea, lunch, afternoon tea," he said. "If it's raining they don't work at all." The fact was, it rained almost every day.

The longshoremen simply refused to make any exception to their standard work rules for the war effort or for these Americans who had come to their country to defend them. So we did it ourselves, and we did it right.

I was now a first lieutenant and my battalion's intelligence officer. Wild Bill McKelvy picked me for the job, for reasons only he understood. My first assignment: steal a jeep belonging to our regiment's First Battalion, commanded by McKelvy's pal, Lieutenant Colonel Lenard "Charlie" Cresswell. Our transport ships—the *Barnett* for them, the *McCawley* for us—were docked next to each other and were both being unloaded so we could sort everything out for combat loading. The jeep was parked on the cluttered dock, waiting to be combat-loaded. "I have a job for you," said McKelvy, "but be silent about it."

My men—they had larceny in their hearts—loved the challenge of the assignment. They pulled a small derrick into position, poised within striking distance of Cresswell's jeep. When one of those rare moments came along when no one was looking, we hitched the jeep to the derrick and swept it up to the deck of our own ship. With a paint can and a stencil, one of my men effected a quick transformation from First Battalion to Third, and, when he was finished, signaled to an ally down in the hold. The jeep was lowered away. Creswell may have heard rumors about what had happened, because he nursed suspicions about his missing jeep for months. But he never could prove a thing.

Not everyone in New Zealand was as obstinate as the longshoremen. Other workers, many of them women, put up what Vandegrift called "a good little camp" for the Marines on the hills outside of town. We settled down for what we thought would be a reasonable amount of time to train ourselves for the fighting to come.

Vandegrift's immediate senior officer was Vice Admiral Robert Ghormley, commander, South Pacific, or, in the predictable acronym, COMSOPAC. We hadn't been in New Zealand a week when Ghormley summoned Vandegrift to a meeting in Auckland at the admiral's headquarters.

"Vandegrift," the admiral said, "I have some very disconcerting news." The strategists in Washington, he explained in what Vandegrift thought was a brusque, harassed manner, wanted us to seize Tulagi and Guadalcanal in the Solomon Islands, northwest of New Zealand. And we were told we would land there on August 1, just thirty-seven days away.

Ghormley wouldn't be up to the job in the weeks ahead, but, amazingly, we would.

It's unlikely many of us knew just how desperate our situation was. The Japanese already had seized Wake, Guam, Singapore, the Philippines, and the Dutch East Indies. Late in January of 1942, they seized Rabaul, on New Britain, and Bougainville in the northern Solomons, and turned Rabaul into a very powerful advance base. As soon as Rabaul was secured, the chief Japanese strategist, Admiral Isoroku Yamamoto, sent the Kure Third Special Naval Landing Force to seize Tulagi with its fine natural harbor. Yamamoto saw Tulagi as a key naval and air base from which to launch the invasion of Port Moresby, in New Guinea, and the subsequent drive to Australia and New Zealand. Tulagi fell like a ripe plum on May 3, and soon base units began pouring in.

But it wasn't until July 1 that Japanese troops and labor battalions landed on Guadalcanal to build an airfield. The great naval battles—Coral Sea on May 7 and 8, almost a draw, and the key American victory at Midway, June 4 and 5, in which four Japanese aircraft carriers were sunk—were major factors in slowing down the Japanese timetable.

An airfield on Guadalcanal, though, was bad news, and so the service chiefs in Washington decided it was time to counterattack, and Tulagi and Guadalcanal would be the targets. Though I was now a lowly intelligence officer, I had never heard of these islands. Nor had hardly anybody else. What we needed was information. What we needed, especially, were maps.

Tulagi and Guadalcanal, we learned, had been under the political control of the British Solomon Islands Protectorate, with a resident commissioner in a small headquarters building on Tulagi, a tiny island just north of Guadalcanal itself. They had all fled in advance of the Japanese landing.

Guadalcanal, we would discover, was a strange place, stretching east and west some ninety miles, with a spiny backbone of precipitous mountains rising as high as eight thousand feet. Along the center of the north coast the mountains lowered to give way to a series of large kunai grass plains and coastal coconut plantations interspersed with countless streams and rivers. It was very hot and very wet. I thought it was the most beautiful place I had ever seen; I still think so.

The natives—we were warned that up until recently they had maintained a keen appetite for "big pig," meaning human flesh—fished and hunted, and didn't much like the Japanese or, when the time came to meet them, the Americans.

But maps we didn't have. Vandegrift sent his chief intelligence officer, Frank Goettge, to Australia to see what he could come up with. He returned with good news: staff officers for General Douglas MacArthur, never a friend of the Marine Corps, promised to send us some maps and to fly some photo-reconnaissance missions over the islands to give us a mosaic picture of the beaches.

It wasn't until 1948 that the Marines learned what had happened. In fact, MacArthur kept his word and Army Air Corps Colonel Karl Polifka did fly the photo mission and produced two strips of the north shore of the island. Getting them to the map plant was given A-1 priority, but they were diverted for ten days "due to a whim of the [Army] transportation officer at Townsville [in northern Australia]."

The photo strips did finally make their way to Melbourne, and the maps were actually produced. But, the Army admitted in 1948, they were lost "in the tremendous pile of boxes incident to the organizing of the base establishment" for South Pacific operations.

Goettge also returned from Australia with eight civilians who had spent time on Guadalcanal. One of them, Vandegrift wrote, produced a crude map of the north coast of Guadalcanal which would become the one map we relied on when the invasion began. The problem was, it was mostly inaccurate, leading to the monumental confusion over the identity of the rivers on the north coast that got me in so much trouble with McKelvy.

We finally sailed from Wellington—waving farewell to the longshoremen—on July 22. But our destination wasn't Guadalcanal. Not yet. We were on our way to Fiji for a dress rehearsal landing practice—gorgeous beaches, tall palms, and sharks.

We appeared off Koro, one of the Fiji islands, on July 26. It was there that Vandegrift met for the first time with the major players in this operation—Admirals Frank Jack Fletcher, John McCain, Thomas Kinkaid, Richmond Kelly Turner, and Victor Crutchley. But Ghormley missed the meeting—a huge mistake, historians say—and sent an aide, Rear Admiral Daniel J. Callaghan, instead.

Fletcher presided, and Vandegrift, who had never met the man before, worried that he seemed so tired and nervous. "To my surprise," said Vandegrift, "he seemed to lack knowledge of or interest in the forthcoming operation. He quickly let us know that he did not think it would succeed."

He infuriated Vandegrift—made "my Dutch blood boil"—by stating he would leave the Guadalcanal area with his aircraft carriers and warships two days after the landing because he didn't want to risk having any of his ships sunk. The Marines needed air cover for at least five days to make the landing, and Fletcher had no intention of giving it to us.

We didn't know about the unfortunate talks between the men who would lead us in this first critical campaign in the Pacific. We did know the dress rehearsal was a disaster. There were coral reefs that threatened to wreck the landing boats we would need for the real landing, and we had to call off much of the rehearsal to save them. What I remembered most about Koro were the sharks, and they were huge brutes. One of them cruised lazily around our ship, seemingly licking his chops. It was at times like these that I wondered what a nice lad from West Chester was doing out here.

We finally set sail for Guadalcanal on July 31—nineteen thousand Marines aboard twenty-three transports. We sailed on the old *McCawley*, Cresswell's jeep in the hold and Vandegrift himself on the bridge.

4

Making a Landing

For all our memorization of Fleet Training Publication No. 167, we didn't need a word of it when we landed on Red Beach on the north coast of Guadalcanal on August 7, 1942.

No one was there to meet us.

The trouble was taking place on little Tulagi Island, where "Red Mike" Edson's Raiders were up against fierce opposition from a small force of entrenched Japanese regulars in a small-scale preview of the kinds of fighting the Marines would face on Iwo Jima and Tarawa.

But Guadalcanal was no problem at all. The Fifth Marines came ashore first and we came in fifty minutes later, without a shot being aimed in our direction. It was a lovely mile-long, gently shelving and sandy beach, ideal for a landing. We were puzzled by the stillness. We stared at a wall of jungle just beyond the beach and wondered what it contained. Maybe, we thought, there weren't any Japanese on the island at all.

Our orders were to move across the beach and march a mile or two to a high point we had been told was Mt. Austen. But where the hell was Mt. Austen? All we had was that crude map drawn on mimeograph paper, and it showed we should be moving across a flat plain. But soon we began encountering a series of ridges. They weren't all that high; the problem was they were steep, and because we had been confined so long in cramped quarters aboard the *McCawley,* we weren't in top physical condition.

Distance is based on linear measurement, but this obscures the great importance of the ups and downs in the terrain. Crude maps can be misleading, and our crude map was very misleading. Good maps need to show the up-and-down relief, and not a solid plain colored green that suggests the terrain is flat. That was the case with the north coast of Guadalcanal. From reading our map, we thought the going would be easy, because the map seemed to say so. What we needed were good maps with accurate contour lines, but we never saw maps like that.

To make our job even more difficult, we had to contend with the eight-foot-high kunai grass. We were surrounded by it, putting us in a kind of heat trap and completely blocking our vision of where we were or where we were going. This was turning out to be the classic problem of long marches—the disappearing goal. We kept hoping Mt. Austen would be just over the next ridge, as our useless map suggested it should be, but, of course, it never was. Little did we know that the mountain was more than six miles away.

We crossed one stream early in the day. Clearly, I said, the Ilu. We forded it by driving a sputtering "Jefferson" amphibious tractor into its depths, using it as a bridge. By late afternoon we heard the delightful sound of running water again. We were happy. Colonel McKelvy, who by now was huffing and puffing so badly we were beginning to worry about him, was delighted. "It's the Lunga River," he said. "No," I said, "it isn't." "Look how wide it is," the colonel said; "any damn fool can see it's wider than the stream we crossed earlier." "Deeper, too," I said, "and anyway it was flowing to our left, and the Lunga, should we ever find it, would be flowing downhill towards the north coast, to our right. No doubt of it," I said, in supreme if reckless confidence, "this is the meandering Ilu, again."

That, of course, led to the outburst I remember most about those early days on Guadalcanal. "Jesus wept!" this preposterous man shouted. "Of course it's the Lunga and no damn lieutenant is going to tell me it isn't. More of this kind of talk out of you and we're going to start thinking about a court-martial."

Vandegrift, we learned later, was worried about two of his battalions—the First, from the Fifth Marines, commanded by Lieutenant Colonel

William E. Maxwell, and our battalion, the Third, from the First Marines. Maxwell's battalion, Vandegrift said, was moving so slowly it seemed they were expecting "to encounter the entire imperial army." Vandegrift gave the battalion commander hell (and replaced him a few days later). Vandegrift visited the Fifth Marines command post (CP) and told the regiment's commanding officer, Colonel Leroy Hunt, that he wanted Marines on the banks of the Tenaru River, two miles west, by nightfall. That speeded things up.

Next he visited the CP of my regimental commander, Colonel Clifton B. Cates, to discover that McKelvy and the rest of us from the Third Battalion were "bogged down in an immense rain forest west of the Ilu River." Note, please, he says Ilu River, not the Lunga. "I saw nothing for it but to order Cliff [Cates] to halt and dig in for the night." And so we did, on the banks of the sluggish Ilu River.

The next morning, Vandegrift got his first good look at Mt. Austen, concluding it "obviously lay several miles further inland than reported. We decided to forget about it for the time being. Instead we ordered Cates to shift northwest out of the rain forest"—he means the tall kunai grass—and "then push west to the airfield."

We were nervous because we expected momentarily to run into strong Japanese opposition. But all the "Jesus wepts" were really unnecessary. The Japanese had fled. There weren't that many of them to begin with. They had only occupied Guadalcanal in early July—with Captain Kodoma's Eleventh and Lieutenant Commander Okimura's Thirteenth Naval Billeting Units, and they were busy building an airstrip on the Lunga Point field, utilizing four hundred engineers, five hundred troops, and a thousand naval construction laborers. As soon as our ships opened their bombardment, they headed for the hills.

Once we realized the situation, we advanced to the west along the coast road at our leisure. To me, and to many of us, the biggest surprise was cultural. Our enemy were sybarites! They had abandoned their camps and everything that went with them. The officers, we discovered, lived in a tent city at Kukum with concrete floors, and they had brought with them a perfectly astounding collection of pornography. They had electric lights, steel-covered air-raid shelters, and elaborate concrete privies.

It was my first insight into the mind of the Japanese fighting man. When the battle for Guadalcanal was over, that would be my specialty, for I would be assigned to the Marines' Staff and Command School at Quantico with my regimental intelligence officer, Merrill "Bill" Twining, to teach officer-students from our armed forces and from Allied armies from all over the world what to expect in fighting this ferocious enemy.

Guadalcanal would be a perfect laboratory. First of all, because it was one of the few campaigns in the Pacific in which numbers, equipment, and morale were roughly equal, so that the decisions hung on the tactical skills of the opposing commanders and their respective staffs. Second, because we captured an immense amount of research material from the Japanese in the form of diaries, prisoner interrogations, orders, pep-talk speeches, and letters. I saved much of it, and it is now a part of the records in the Marine Corps Historical Center in Washington.

It would be our conclusion that the Japanese, though brave enough, had serious shortcomings in making war. Their very worst mistake was in underestimating their enemy. While they were building the air base on Guadalcanal, Radio Tokyo was having a fine time. "Where are the United States Marines?" a commentator asked, dripping sarcasm. "The Marines are supposed to be the finest soldiers in the world, but no one has seen them."

Many of the Japanese soldiers and officers believed their own propaganda—that Americans were unable to bear hardship and worshiped only material luxuries which could be seen in American movies. American tactics, their manuals explained, disdained the spiritual element exemplified by Japanese doctrine and relied on material to carry the day. The Yankees, they believed, feared cold steel. Americans themselves, it needs to be said, worried if their own fighting men would be a match for these proud and fanatical warriors from Japan. Guadalcanal would change that.

By all accounts, Japanese soldiers were supposed to be brilliant tacticians, merciless night fighters, capable sharpshooters. Guadalcanal would change that too. They were, we would find, none of these things. They attacked foolishly, closely bunched together, making themselves bull's eyes for our own sharpshooters. They frequently got lost at night and had a terrible time coordinating night attacks. And as for marksmanship, they were second rate. When things went right, they frequently failed to follow up their successes, losing the advantage time and time again. And when things went wrong, as they frequently did, their commanding officers, in the best Bushido warrior tradition, would commit suicide.

My regimental commander, Colonel Cates, a future Marine Corps commandant, would say when the battle was over: "I still claim they are dumb."

Perhaps the Japanese had been lulled by their earlier successes. The basic Japanese division was designed for operations against the Chinese. Rather than make special divisions heavy in firepower for action against the more heavily armed Americans, the Japanese preferred a more flexible system of assigning special units as needed.

What they never expected, we found, was the tenacity and resourcefulness of the individual American fighting man, Marine or, in time, soldier. Nor, until Guadalcanal, had they any idea of the effectiveness of massed American artillery fire.

But the biggest news for us on August 7 was nothing so cosmic as all that. We had turned up the biggest prize of all—a huge supply of beer, sake, and Suntory whiskey. The Marines, needless to say, were jubilant. Before they could wade into the goodies, though, McKelvy stepped forward and impounded all of it. The booze, he said, was off-limits to everyone, officers and men alike. Except, no surprise, himself. For the rest of the time we were on Guadalcanal, McKelvy nipped. He was never actually falling-down drunk. He was always just a little squiffed.

We seized huge amounts of food too—rice, canned Alaskan crab, salmon, mushrooms. What I remember most were the fish heads and the barley. The barley struck us as dull stuff, and we didn't have the nerve to try the fish heads.

Vandegrift couldn't believe the Marines' haul. He described it in a letter to the Marines' commandant, General Thomas Holcomb: "A power house, an alternate one, a radio receiver station with six sets with remote control to a sending unit three miles away, innumerable pieces of machinery such as generators, engines, pumps, etc. 9 Road Rollers, over 100 trucks . . . anti-air guns, loaded and locked—can you beat that? Tons of cement, some fifty or sixty thousand gals. of gas and oil . . . and hundreds of other items."

We named everything we captured for the Japanese premier, General Hideki Tojo. The trucks, then, were the Tojo Truck Works. We even picked up an ice-making machine. It became the Tojo Ice Company.

The booty included what turned out to be a superior Japanese surgical kit. The Marines used the Japanese instruments for the rest of the campaign. The Japanese had a better hospital tent, too, and even their bug spray worked better than ours.

When he wrote that letter to his commandant, Vandegrift was glowing with confidence. It lasted just a few hours. Toward dark on August 8, he was summoned back to the *McCawley* to meet Admiral Turner.

Vandegrift thought it was just a routine meeting to discuss ways to improve the chaotic situation in sorting out supplies from the ships on the beach. It was more than that: Turner, and his sidekick, the unfortunate Ghormley, had bad news. Enemy planes, they said, were preparing to attack the Navy's ships off the Guadalcanal coast, so Vice Admiral Frank J. Fletcher had decided that the Navy, short of fuel, was being forced to withdraw its carriers and other big ships, even earlier than the time set at the first conference off Fiji, leaving behind a number of cruisers and destroyers. Turner said he planned to remove all the transport and cargo vessels as well; many of them still were waiting to be unloaded.

"This was the Koro [Fiji] conference relived," Vandegrift wrote, "except that Fletcher was running away 12 hours earlier than he had already threatened during our unpleasant meeting [on Fiji]. We all knew his fuel could not have been running low since he refueled in the Fijis—a tidbit of knowledge that solved nothing. Here was a *fait accompli,* and we knew it."

The Marines, Vandegrift now understood, would fight this battle alone.

We would need that captured barley to survive, and maybe if things got worse, those gross fish heads.

In fact, things did get worse—fast.

Approaching Guadalcanal was a Japanese naval task force, led by five heavy cruisers, a light cruiser, and one destroyer. Commanding the Japanese force, aboard the heavy cruiser *Chokai,* was a brilliant sailor, Rear Admiral Gunichi Mikawa. Waiting for Mikawa was an Allied squadron consisting of four American and two Australian heavy cruisers, supported by two light cruisers and eight destroyers, a vastly superior force, all under the overall command of the American, Turner, and the direct command of Australian Rear Admiral Victor A. C. Crutchley.

Vice Admiral Fletcher would have been there with his two big fleet carriers, but of course he had withdrawn them on the eve of the battle in a decision that still draws criticism.

During the night of August 8–9, Admiral Mikawa steamed down "the Slot" and launched a surprise attack on Crutchley's squadron off Savo Island that produced the worst defeat suffered by the American Navy in World War II. He attacked first with torpedoes, hitting both *Canberra* and *Chicago,* and then turned on his searchlights and opened up with his big guns on the rest of the Allied ships at almost point-blank range. Four Allied cruisers were sunk and another badly damaged, with the loss of more than a thousand American and Australian sailors; two Japanese ships were damaged, slightly, with the loss of 129 Japanese seamen.

Those of us on shore watched the whole thing—we had front-row seats for a thrilling sea battle. It was a spectacular sight—ships exploding in the rockets' red glare. We had no idea who was winning, at first, but we began to get an inkling when the operators of our radio transmitters reported they couldn't get through to our principal ships. The reason they weren't getting through, of course, was that our big ships were eight fathoms deep.

Now was the key moment—the time to destroy the American landing on Guadalcanal, for the cargo ships were still lying off the island and they were helpless. Instead, Mikawa turned away, in a typical example of the failure of the Japanese to seize the initiative. The death stroke to those of us on Guadalcanal was averted.

Guadalcanal historian Richard B. Frank reckons we were left with 6,075 Marines in the Tulagi-Gavutu-Tanambogo area, including six infantry battalions, and 10,819 Marines, but only five infantry battalions, including my own, on Guadalcanal.

Even though Vandegrift received a Medal of Honor for his performance on Guadalcanal, I'm not sure he's ever been given the credit he deserves for his extraordinary leadership in what was now an extremely perilous time for the United States. But he never flinched. He called his division staff and commanders down through battalion level to his command post the morning of August 9, following the terrible naval disaster, and prepared to give them the bad news.

"Singly or in pairs they straggled to my CP," he wrote later, "a sorry-looking lot with bloodshot eyes and embryonic beards and filthy dungarees. . . . They were tired. Some smoked, others sipped black coffee. . . . Most of them watched the beach and the parade of small boats landing survivors whose semi-naked bodies black from burns and oil of the sunken ships claimed the ministrations of our doctors and corpsmen. Even as they watched, the cruiser *Chicago,* her bow shot away, limped past transports busily hoisting landing craft to their decks [in preparation for making their own departure]."

They were on their way within hours, taking with them most of our heavy equipment, almost all of our barbed wire, and even eighteen hundred men from the Second Marines.

Vandegrift issued his orders: Form a defensive perimeter around the airfield, move the supplies from the beach inside that perimeter, and finish the airfield as rapidly as humanly possible.

But first we had to clean up the beach. It was an incredible mess, a standing rebuke to everything Pete Ellis had taught us in preparation for the writing of Fleet Training Publication No. 167. "The situation is ascribed to a total lack of conception of the number of labor troops required to unload boats and move material off the beach, failure to extend the beach limits earlier in the operation, and, to some extent, lack of control of troops on and in immediate vicinity of the beach," an official investigation concluded. The problem really was the unwillingness of Marines expecting to be attacked momentarily by the Japanese to put their weapons down and start moving boxes.

In preparing his defense, Vandegrift put four of his battalions into the line, with McKelvy and our Third Battalion helping to anchor the eastern section. McKelvy's pal, "Charlie" Creswell, and his First Battalion, and a light-tank company, represented all the reserves Vandegrift had on Guadalcanal.

Vandegrift worried about an attack from the sea, so most of his .30-caliber machine guns and 37mm anti-tank guns were deployed to cover the beach. The artillery—those 75s and 105s from the Eleventh Marines that would be so devastating—were bunched to the south of the airfield. A battery of four 90mm anti-aircraft guns was positioned at the edge of the airfield too.

It was at about this time we discovered we were not alone with the Japanese on Guadalcanal. We had "natives" too. The Japanese already had made an effort to put some of them to work in a program they called "applicants for forced labor." The natives, a manual we captured noted, were to submit to thirty days' forced labor, working from five in the morning until seven at night for one and a half pounds of rice and a stick of tobacco a day. Those whose behavior was exemplary would receive a good conduct badge in addition to their official resident's badge. The exceptional workers would be made chiefs and given several "little chiefs" to boss around.

Despite these inducements, perhaps handsome by Japanese standards, the natives' desire for this kind of highly programmed work, never particularly strong under any circumstances, cooled very quickly. They took to the hills.

The most dangerous of the Japanese officers was a man named Ishimoto. He had worked as a carpenter on Tulagi for years, though he was no doubt already in the pay of the Japanese navy. He returned with the first Japanese landing force in the islands and led a group of forty

troops that scoured the villages looking for troublemakers. He particularly mistrusted two priests, Fathers Henry Oude-Engberink and Arthur
C. Duhamel, and several nuns serving with them, all missionary members of the Society of Mary. They were all stationed at Ruavatu. Ishimoto
believed they knew more than they would say about American dispositions, but they insisted that because they were religious missionaries,
they were neutral. So they refused to answer questions, and when one of
the nuns tried to make an escape, Ishimoto seized a rifle from one of his
men and bayoneted Father Duhamel in the belly. The rest were starved
and tortured for a week before they were all killed. Ishimoto left the disemboweled bodies as an example to the natives.

Up in those hills, too, on Guadalcanal and other islands, was an
absolutely amazing bunch of people called coastwatchers, most of them
Australian government officials and retired planters, mixed with a few
missionaries. Solomon Islands coastwatchers—men such as Captain W.
F. Martin Clemens on Guadalcanal and Jack Reed on Bougainville—
radioed priceless information on the movement of Japanese warships,
planes, and infantry.

Working with Captain Clemens on Guadalcanal were a number of
natives from what had been the Solomon Islands Protectorate Armed
Constabulary. Best of them all was Jacob Charles Vouza, forty-two years
old at the time of our landing and a retired sergeant major in the
Constabulary. He first made his mark on August 7, the day of the landing, when he rescued a downed Navy pilot from the aircraft carrier *Wasp*,
bringing him safely into the Marine lines.

Vouza liked what he saw of the Marines and volunteered to scout
behind the enemy lines for us. He was captured while spying on enemy
lookout stations. After the Japanese found a small American flag in his
loincloth, they tied Vouza to a tree and tried to extract information about
our plans and dispositions from him. The sinister Ishimoto was there,
and he fingered Vouza as a longtime member of the local Constabulary.
But Vouza told them nothing, and so he was bayoneted a dozen or more
times and left to die.

Somehow, though, he managed to untie the knots and make his way
several miles, bleeding profusely, to the Marine perimeter. I was one of
the first Marines to see him, crawling on his hands and knees on the
trail along the shoreline. I was a very green officer, and I had never seen
anything like this. Who in the world was this strange figure? When it
became apparent he was trying to help us, it fell upon me to offer him

the Marines' official welcome. What astonishment! I felt a little like Stanley greeting Dr. Livingstone. To my further astonishment, this fierce-looking character spoke in English that seemed to have a trace of an Oxford accent. (Mostly, though, the natives spoke in pidgin English. One of them, I recall, had spotted a Japanese gun. What size? we asked. "All same big beer bottle," we were told. Easy—75mm.)

But Vouza had no desire to linger; he wanted to report to someone in charge, and so he moved on to headquarters to announce truly important news: The reinforced Japanese, he said, were preparing to attack.

Vouza stuck with us the whole time we were on Guadalcanal, even seeing us off, rendering heroic and important work. Vandegrift personally gave him a Silver Star. The British gave him the George Medal and, in 1979, he was knighted by Queen Elizabeth II. He died, a gallant old man, in 1984.

5

Meeting the Enemy

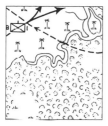 When we invaded Guadalcanal, the senior Japanese commander on the island was Captain Kodoma of the Eleventh Naval Billeting Unit. He was awakened by the crash of exploding naval shells and the whine of attacking dive-bombers.

Kodoma studied the situation and concluded this was just another American hit-and-run raid. Seeing no point in exposing his men to this sort of thing, he ordered them to leave their comfortable base on Lunga Point and move to a safer spot in the jungle ravines to the west.

By the time he reached the Matanikau River he saw that American troops were approaching Lunga Point in landing barges. Maybe, he thought, this wasn't a hit-and-run raid after all. So he composed a dispatch to his superiors in Rabaul in which he chronicled a heroic resistance to the American landing and said he and his command had been pushed westward by overwhelming numbers.

Kodoma's dispatch caused consternation in Rabaul. The easy thing was to send Japanese warships to the islands, and that led to Admiral Mikawa's stunning victory at Savo Island. The harder part was finding a military force to challenge the Marines' unexpected landing.

The task was given to General Harukichi Hyakutake's Seventeenth Army, which had been preparing to invade southeastern New Guinea. His army consisted chiefly of the Second and Thirty-eighth Infantry Divisions, an independent regiment, and a brigade, heavily supported by two heavy field artillery regiments, three anti-aircraft, two anti-tank, and two mortar battalions, plus the usual service units, such as field hospitals, stevedore companies, and engineering regiments.

It was a powerhouse force—on paper. But it was scattered, and there was no way Hyakutake could pull it together until late in October. But Hyakutake was told he couldn't wait that long—recapturing Guadalcanal was far too important, and it had to be done quickly.

Enter, then, the extraordinary figure of Colonel Kiyono Ichiki and his crack Twenty-eighth Regiment, known more familiarly as the Ichiki Detachment. Ichiki was one of the great characters in the Japanese army. He had been an instructor in the Imperial Army's infantry school, and it had been his impetuosity in the "Marco Polo Bridge incident" in 1937 that helped to ignite Japan's war with China. Guadalcanal historian Richard Frank notes that "Ichiki firmly shared the widely held view in the Imperial Army at this time that night attacks with swords and bayonets— the traditional tactic of the Imperial Army—would easily secure success against American forces."

Ichiki was a firebrand. Luckily for us he was also a fool.

It had been the Japanese command's intention to use Ichiki's Detachment to occupy Midway Island. But after the American naval victory off that island, Ichiki's men were basically in the unemployed class. They were on their way home to Tokyo when the Marines landed on Guadalcanal. Hyakutake wired Ichiki to put about immediately and take himself and his regiment to Guadalcanal.

It wasn't only Ichiki who was a fool here. It was the entire Japanese command. Why did they believe that Ichiki and his detachment of twenty-five hundred men could defeat ten thousand Marines? Well, they thought they had evidence that American morale was low. The initial American attack on Lunga Point against poor Captain Kodoma and his outnumbered billeting troops had seemed extremely cautious (partly due to the slow pace of a single battalion, whose commander was soon relieved). The Americans wouldn't go anywhere without heavy artillery barrages to prepare the way. They were not yet using the airfield, though it appeared to be finished. And every night, the green American troops fired off prodigious amounts of ammunition at ghostly enemies in the jungle. Truly, the Japanese figured, a spineless lot.

By August 15, Ichiki had landed at Truk. Because of transportation difficulties, he split his force into two echelons. The first, consisting of nine hundred men and himself, set off for Guadalcanal at 7 a.m. on August 17 aboard six destroyers under the command of Captain Torajiro Sato. They were put ashore at 1 a.m. on August 19 between Taivu and Koli Points and promptly began their march on Lunga Point to seize the airfield in one surprise blow. The second echelon wasn't due to arrive until August 24, when its only job would be to mop up behind Ichiki and his victorious first echelon. So, in fact, the Japanese were sending nine hundred men against ten thousand Marines.

While Ichiki's men marched toward the airfield, three of Captain Sato's destroyers began what appeared to be a leisurely bombardment of American positions on Tulagi. This was interrupted by the arrival of three American B-17 bombers that released a stick of bombs on the Japanese warships. Somewhat surprisingly—for the B-17 attacks were rarely successful—one of the bombs hit the *Hagikaze* and killed thirty-three Japanese sailors.

The objective of the Japanese, it seemed clear enough, was the sandspit at the mouth of what we thought was the Tenaru River (it really was Alligator Creek). The west bank was defended by Lieutenant Colonel Edwin A. Pollock's Second Battalion, linking up with our Third Battalion a thousand yards or so to the west.

Ichiki called his commanders to a meeting at midnight and outlined his plan, though it hardly seems to add up to a plan at all. What he intended to do, he told his officers, was open fire with his 70mm battalion guns, heavy machine guns, and grenade dischargers in the coconut grove on the east bank, and then launch his infantry in a sudden shock attack across the sandspit. Thereafter, he intended to move against the airfield. The whole thing would be simple enough—requiring, he said, "just one brush of the armored sleeve."

Ichiki fired a green flare at 2 a.m. to signal the charge. Screaming and yelling at the top of their lungs, they rushed across the sandspit. The Marines responded with rifle and machine-gun fire, cutting down dozens of the Japanese troops. Even worse were the canister rounds fired by the 37mm anti-tank guns. The survivors kept coming, reaching the barbed wire thirty yards in front of the Marine positions. Some of them, waving bayonets, broke through the barbed wire and engaged in hand-to-hand combat with the Marines.

For the Marines, there were innumerable instances of heroism. One machine gunner, Private John Rivers, killed dozens of the enemy and was still firing when he was killed. His place was taken by Corporal Lee Diamond until he was wounded. Then a third Marine, Private Albert A. Schmid, from Philadelphia, took over the machine gun and kept firing even after he was blinded by an exploding grenade.

Colonel Cates, the regimental commander, ordered the deadly 75mm guns from the Eleventh Marines to lay down concentrated fire on the Japanese position on the sandspit. If you had to devise a way to get a lot of people killed very quickly, you couldn't think of a better way than a banzai charge. The carnage was terrible.

General Vandegrift, in touch by telephone with the action from Cates's CP, took his part, too; he commanded Lieutenant Colonel Cresswell's First Battalion to go upstream, ford the river, and attack Ichiki's men from the rear. "The movement," an official Marine Corps monograph of the battle says, "was an unqualified success."

A few of Ichiki's men tried to swim around the sandbar to get at the Marine positions. They were picked off, one by one. Others tried to get away in small boats. But American aircraft—they had only arrived the day before—appeared now, and they sank the boats.

My own Colonel McKelvy was beside himself with frustration, for our battalion figured in almost no part of the action. Worse, "Charlie" Cresswell and our sister battalion played a key role, coming out of reserve status to do it.

McKelvy had never figured out quite what to do with me—I think it may have been my Ivy League status. For reasons of his own, he believed we were different from other people. So, he left me pretty much on my own with my intelligence section.

That's why I was able to witness the bloody results of the slaughter of Ichiki's Detachment. It was a grisly sight—the smell was terrible, too— with the sandspit dotted with the protruding heads of dead and maybe a few wounded Japanese soldiers. I watched as one of our tanks crossed the river and proceeded to cruise back and forth, crushing what life there might have been on that beach and in the coconut grove. I have never forgotten it.

Vandegrift, it turned out, had offered Cates that platoon of four light tanks to, in the general's words, "finish off the action." Vandegrift said "it was a slaughter," and it was. He noted that "the rear of the tanks looked like meat grinders," and they did. In a letter to Commandant

Holcomb, Vandegrift said, "I have never heard or read of this kind of fighting. These people refuse to surrender. The wounded will wait until the men come up to examine them and blow themselves and the other fellow to pieces with a hand grenade."

As the remnants of his command were being slaughtered, Ichiki burned the precious regimental colors and then, true to the spirit of Bushido, joined his adjutant in ceremonial suicide.

So was fought the misnamed Battle of the Tenaru (it should have been the Battle of Alligator Creek, but even that had its problems, for there were no alligators here, only crocodiles, though I never saw an alligator or a crocodile on Guadalcanal).

"We beat the Japanese at the Tenaru," Vandegrift wrote. "In but hours its psychological effect grew out of all proportion to its physical dimensions. Yesterday the Jap seemed something almost superhuman, a kind of mechanical juggernaut that swept inexorably through the Philippines, the Dutch East Indies, over the beaches at Guam and Wake Island, through the jungles of New Guinea. . . . But today *we* had beaten the Jap. The Jap no longer seemed superhuman. The Jap was a physical thing, a soldier in uniform, carrying a rifle and firing machine guns and mortars and charging stupidly against barbed wire and rifles and machine guns. We stopped this Jap. . . ."

The Ichiki attack was just plain dumb. Though the Imperial Army's staff had never actually authorized it, they hadn't discouraged it either. The fact that eight hundred of Japan's most skilled fighting men were slaughtered in a matter of two hours speaks for itself. Marine losses in the engagement came to forty-three dead and seventy-one wounded.

In reporting the results, the Japanese said: "The attack of the Ichiki detachment has not been entirely successful."

Guadalcanal was a curious battleground. We would be the subject of intensive banzai attacks one day, after which everything would be routine for a week or two at a time. It was nothing like the around-the-clock fighting that marked Iwo Jima and Tarawa.

We had a daily routine. It would begin at 6 a.m. with chow lines and anti-malaria doses of Atabrine. Then it would be time for McKelvy's executive officer (until September 25, anyway), Major Walker A. Reaves, to do his stuff. Reaves was a martinet, and he was very good at it. He would assign all of us chores after breakfast—work parties to enlarge our defensive positions, for example.

McKelvy was obsessed with the importance of field sanitation. It was no doubt something he had picked up during the time he spent in such places as Nicaragua and Cuba. We buried our waste every day and, at McKelvy's insistence, marked each spot with a small sign noting the date the pit was filled and the outfit responsible. Maybe he wasn't as crazy as we thought—at least we didn't suffer from dysentery as badly as some of the other units.

God knows, Bill McKelvy was a character. We had this peculiar adversarial relationship with him, and most of the time he seemed to relish it. "Think you're going to keep on living?" he would ask Captain Dumas, whom he loved to kid (and vice versa). "You're gonna die. You're *all* gonna die—even me, you bastard!"

But was he crazy? Maybe. Madness was never far from McKelvy's consciousness. He didn't socialize with us very much, but sometimes, in the evening, when it was obvious he had been drinking, he would drop by and tell us he had been treated years earlier at St. Elizabeth's Hospital, a mental institution in Washington, D.C. He seemed proud of it. "Nutty as a fruitcake," he would say about himself.

He hinted that his relationship with his father, the original "Wild Bill," had not been a happy one, and that he had spent a lifetime trying to meet his father's expectations. Some nights he thought of himself as a grand strategist, and lamented the days when he had designed a series of attacks against major Japanese bases. One of them involved taking Truk, the great naval base. None of his ideas, he said, had been taken seriously.

We played jokes on him, all the time, and Dumas was the No. 1 jokester. One night, when we were camped along the Matanikau, the stillness was broken by what appeared to be a Japanese soldier speaking English. "Good evening, Colonel McKelvy," the voice, somewhere out there near the sandspit, said.

McKelvy was drawn in, hook, line, and sinker. "Jesus wept!" he roared. "The son of a bitch knows my name!" He leaped to his feet, ordering me to check our ground communication. Send a runner to division headquarters to alert them to the possibility we faced an attack, he bellowed.

As the minutes ticked by, and nothing seemed to be happening, a few of us began laughing. And when McKelvy finally took note that Dumas was missing, the truth swept over him. He had the good grace to laugh, too. Dumas was his favorite, and he always received redemption.

Another time, Dumas put on some captured Japanese sandals—they left a distinctive footprint—and, when McKelvy was asleep, walked in them up to his tent, shuffled around in the dirt, then walked away, back toward the jungle. When McKelvy awoke early the next morning, he hardly had time to stretch before he saw the footprints. "Jesus wept!" he roared. "The bastard walked right up to my tent!"

Guadalcanal was a sociable place. During the day, when we had nothing better to do, we would gather by the huge trunk of a banyan tree which had fallen into the Lunga River. It was great for washing clothes, checking the latest gossip, and cleaning up our feet. This was important, for the Marines were susceptible to jungle rot, and this odious condition was universally abhorred, though some of the men seemed reluctant to do much to avoid it.

I would sometimes show up at the banyan tree to launder two or more of the several muslin sheets I had managed to sneak ashore when we came to the island. They were the subject of some derision, but I had the last laugh. No matter where headquarters moved our tents, I slept on clean sheets every night. I'm not sure anyone else who served on Guadalcanal can make the same boast.

Evening was the best time. The sun had set and the blazing temperatures had receded. A light breeze would be coming in from offshore. Now was the cocktail hour. We used canned grapefruit juice as the base, to which we would add several squeezes of toothpaste. Doc Keyserling, the battalion surgeon, supplied us with medicinal alcohol. I found Pepsodent, grapefruit juice, and medicinal alcohol quite tolerable.

McKelvy avoided us most of the time—he had his own booze supply, which he never shared with anyone. We would rattle the ice—courtesy of the Tojo Ice Company, of course—in our cups to taunt him.

McKelvy got his own revenge. He had this sergeant who used to toady up to him all the time, and he played the harmonica. He and the sergeant would get together, night after night, and sing the same three songs over and over again. McKelvy's favorite was, "Come, Josephine, in My Flying Machine." We heard it so many times we thought we would all go mad.

Even so, we knew what was coming. Japanese ships were constantly offshore, shelling Marine positions. Even a couple of their submarines fired a few shots at us. And Japanese planes were overhead all the time. One of them, Washing Machine Charlie, would head our way every night, just to make sure we didn't get a sound night's sleep.

The Lunga Point airfield, now called Henderson Field, was operational, and our own fighters rose from it every day to challenge the Japanese aircraft. We could watch the dogfights as they took place overhead, cheering as one of our Wildcats shot down one of their Zeros, moaning when a Zero shot down one of ours. The Zero was a first-class fighting machine, faster and more maneuverable than our Wildcat. But we always had an advantage—those wonderful coastwatchers. Time after time, they gave us enough advance warning of a wave of Japanese planes approaching to allow us to climb above the Zeros and come at them in speed dives. It was busy work. On one day, August 29, the Japanese carrier *Ryujo* launched an attack, and lost sixteen aircraft (we lost four).

The two navies fought another battle, called the Battle of the Eastern Solomons, on August 24 and 25, complete with battleships and big aircraft carriers. It wasn't a loss this time, but it wasn't a great victory either. One of the problems was that Admiral Fletcher had withdrawn one of his big carriers, *Wasp*, for refueling, and so what could have been a big superiority in American ships over the enemy was lost. For us, the big news was that a convoy carrying fresh troops to resume the ground attack on Guadalcanal was forced to turn back.

Unable to push a convoy through to Guadalcanal, the Japanese turned to late-night dashes by destroyers loaded with troops to do the job. On August 29, for example, four destroyers landed nine hundred men at Tassafaronga. Two nights later, destroyers landed twelve hundred men from Major General Kiyotake Kawaguchi's brigade at Tasimboko.

But it wasn't always easy. American planes took a deadly toll, to the point that the Japanese changed tactics and attempted to bring troops ashore by barge. The ineffable Colonel Akinosuku Oka—he would be the Marines' best friend in the days ahead—lost hundreds of men trying to reach Guadalcanal.

Kawaguchi's brigade came fresh to the Seventeenth Army from its victorious campaign in Borneo, and at the time of our landing on Guadalcanal was busy at Palau rehearsing for the New Guinea operation. The brigade was composed of Oka's 124th Regiment, three infantry battalions, an infantry battalion from another unit, and the orphaned second echelon of the Ichiki Detachment, plus artillery, anti-aircraft guns, and engineers—a total force of about sixty-two hundred men.

Even before he reached Guadalcanal, Kawaguchi sketched out a plan. Oka would land with his 124th Regiment near the Matanikau River, west of the American lines, while the rest of the force landed, like the Ichiki unit, between Taivu and Koli Points. This time, there would be no rash advance, but rather a slow, steady, secret movement through the jungle to the south of our perimeter. In a coordinated blow, Oka's force would hit the Marines from the west, while the real powerhouse punch was being delivered along a spiny ridge south of the airfield. The second echelon of the Ichiki Detachment was given the honor of attacking across the Tenaru (further upstream from the sandspit this time) in order to put to rest the departed souls of Ichiki and his first echelon.

But, by now, the Marines were stronger, too, for "Red Mike" Edson—he had red hair—and his Raiders had been transferred to Guadalcanal from Tulagi. Edson was a cold, compelling soldier, with a brilliant grasp of what well-trained Marines could accomplish. On September 8, he took his Raiders by boat to make a landing behind Japanese lines at Tasimboko, on Taivu Point. After a fierce little fight, they drove the Japanese defenders away and then calmly began destroying Japanese supplies and weapons—and packing up top-secret documents. Historian Frank says the Marines returned home with twenty-one cases of beer and seventeen half-gallon flasks of sake. Edson lost two men killed. A Japanese officer said the whole episode was "daring and insulting."

Back at headquarters, Edson told Vandegrift this was a serious Japanese concentration, and that an attack would begin soon. Where would it come from? Edson pointed a finger at a grassy ridge clearly marked out on an aerial map. "This looks like a good approach," he said.

The ridge would in a few days' time be known, then and forever after, as Edson's Ridge, the scene of the sharpest, and most decisive, fighting in the Guadalcanal campaign.

6

Fighting the Enemy

We played a major role in the decisive events that took place starting September 13, for we were the object of a banzai charge ourselves. McKelvy couldn't have been more pleased, helped in no small measure by the fact he was interviewed after it was all over by International News Service correspondent Richard Tregaskis.

I was pretty pleased with myself, too. "They attacked us in the jungle with much trooping and hollering and shouting of 'Banzai!,'" I wrote Dad and Margaret in particularly gung ho manner. "The officers waved their samurai swords like a bunch of kids but the net result was that instead of our men retreating they jumped out of their foxholes and scared the wits out of the Japs by tearing at them with knives and bayonets. I suppose the Japs have been so used to other armies running away when they shouted and made faces that it never occurred to them they'd really have to fight. No kidding—our men are superb fighters and they'll close in for the kill every time. A bloodthirsty bunch—they'll use knives and bayonets on the Japanese whenever they can.

"The Japs shout 'Devil Marines!' at us. You can read the papers for the number of Jap corpses piled up."

I mentioned in this letter the exploits of my close friend, Lieutenant Joseph A. Terzi of Little Neck, Long Island. Joe was a first-class athlete—a football star at Niagara University in upstate New York and a member in 1941 of the top-ranked Quantico Marines team that featured the University of Pennsylvania's all-American, Francis X. Reagan, at tailback.

Joe "had become trapped behind the Jap lines and we had given him up for lost but he came in the next morning," I wrote. "Had spent the night under a log the Japs were using for a bridge."

McKelvy tells the same story in his interview with Tregaskis that became a part later of the correspondent's best-selling book, *Guadalcanal Diary*: "That morning—that was the 14th—we were given a reserve of six tanks. There was high grass across from our positions and we were afraid the Japs were lying doggo in there. While the tanks were in, one of our lieutenants jumped on one of the tanks. He was a Lieutenant Turzai"—a misspelling—"who had been wounded by shrapnel and stayed surrounded by Japs all night."

Not only was Terzi behind the Japanese lines; he was smack in the middle of a Japanese command post. He was fearful he would give away his position—just a cough would have done it. So all night long he stayed there as motionless as possible under that big banyan tree.

When the sun came up the morning of the fourteenth, Joe was spotted by the Japanese. "But instead of running he made a face at the Japs and lunged at them," I wrote my father and stepmother. "One look at Joe would be enough to scare a whole Jap division out of its wits. He's a mean looking customer, especially with a three days' beard." Joe ran right through some machine-gun positions just in time to spot the advancing American light tanks. Joe yelled at them and waved his arms frantically. He grimaced and growled, hoping to scare the stunned Japanese away. His behavior simply immobilized the enemy. Joe finally climbed aboard one of the tanks and made his getaway.

"I scared the hell out of them," he said with immense satisfaction.

McKelvy told Tregaskis about the machine guns Joe had run through; they were located near a shack in the high grass. "Later in the day," McKelvy said, "we sent the tanks after them. They accomplished their mission, with some losses."

"Some losses" was an understatement. The tanks were sent back, following the exact same route—"folly," according to historian Richard Frank—and this time the Japanese were waiting for them. They destroyed three of the tanks with their anti-tank guns. Crews from two of the tanks escaped, but the crew of the third died when their tank toppled down a ravine and overturned. Another tank was disabled.

Joe's turn came the next year, on December 26, when he was killed during the Marines' campaign at Cape Gloucester, in western New Britain.

We didn't know it at the time, but we had been attacked by the Kuma ("Bear") Battalion, the Right Wing Unit in Japanese planning, commanded by Major Eiji Mizuno. This was actually Ichiki's second echelon, recently arrived on Guadalcanal and facing no better prospects than the ill-fated first echelon. These 550 soldiers had been given the honor of advancing against our position on Alligator Creek because it wasn't far from where the first echelon had been destroyed. Their victory, they were told, would give "repose to the departed souls of the Ichiki Detachment commander and men."

We had formed a thin defensive line running almost four thousand yards, north to south, with L Company on the left flank, I Company in the center, and K Company on the right flank. The rifle companies were supported by three machine-gun platoons and our 81mm mortar platoon. But we were so thin that there was no one positioned for a stretch of three hundred yards or more to the south, meaning the Japanese had an open path to Henderson Field to our rear if they could only take advantage of it.

But they had launched their bayonet attack directly against K Company's lines—I was perched on a good spot nearby and saw and heard it all—and were destroyed. Sword-waving Major Mizuno died in the initial attack. The surviving members of his unit attacked again the night of the fourteenth, but with little conviction. They made an even weaker attempt on the fifteenth. We pushed them back both times without any losses of our own.

What was left of the Kuma Battalion gave up the fight and turned back in an effort to catch up with the main Japanese force, but they became lost in the jungle. Historian Frank says they wandered aimlessly for three entire weeks before they were rescued, "losing all their weapons and becoming severely malnourished."

Why the Kuma Battalion insisted on making a frontal assault on our front lines remains a mystery. If they'd done some decent patrolling, they would have found that breach in our lines to the left, and the way would have been clear to Henderson Field.

Our action was generally overlooked in the reporting of the more dramatic fighting at Bloody Ridge, but historian William H. Bartsch, in the

September 1997 issue of the *Marine Corps Gazette,* gave us belated credit. "Crucial Battle Ignored," the headline says.

It was never a necessity for the Japanese to capture Henderson Field, though of course that would have been a supreme achievement. All they had to do was put it out of action, by bombs from aircraft, shells from ships, or heavy artillery from strategic locations. Colonel Cates, our regimental commander, worried all the time about the problem that would be presented to us by heavy Japanese guns high on Mt. Austen. "They would have direct observation of the airfield and many of our batteries and it would be almost impossible to operate planes or fire our artillery," he wrote in his unpublished memoirs. "It goes to prove my contention— they are courageous but dumb."

Every day, Navy, Marine, and Army Air Corps aircraft roared away from the little airfield, attacking Zeros and Bettys and anything else the Japanese sent our way in the air. They dive-bombed Japanese destroyers and strafed Japanese barges. It was those bullet-riddled planes that kept the enemy from landing heavy reinforcements of men and supplies.

The attack on our lines had been just a part of a major thrust to capture Henderson Field and put an end to what had now become the major test of arms between Japan and the United States.

Kawaguchi's idea, you will recall, was to push his main body through the dense jungle south of the oval-shaped, fifteen-square-mile Marine perimeter, and carry the day with a well-coordinated attack that would also include the Kuma Battalion against our lines at the eastern edge of the perimeter and Oka's forces at the western edge. Kawaguchi was so certain of success that he had brought his dress-white uniform to wear at the ceremony in which the Americans would surrender.

But the vaunted ability of the Japanese army to move quietly and efficiently, night and day, quickly came unraveled. This little army became lost and confused, and units kept bumping into each other in the night.

Oka wasn't in a preferred position. Because he had landed in the wrong place, he was in no position to command most of the men from his own regiment, the 124th. Three of his battalions were a part of Kawaguchi's command, making the thrust from the south. Oka found himself commanding a mixed collection of regulars, sailors, and construction workers. With them, he was under orders to make a coordinated attack from the west.

Oka was a puzzling character—the very opposite of the stereotype of the highly disciplined, order-taking, courageous Japanese officer. Oka was none of these things—he wasn't disciplined at all, he rarely followed orders, and he showed an aversion for facing his enemy.

Oka had agreed to lead his detachment toward a key bridge west of the airfield and then make an assault to begin at 8 p.m. on September 12 against the airfield itself, to be synchronized with Kawaguchi's thrust from the south (and, of course, the Kuma Battalion's thrust from the east).

The timing for the Japanese should have been perfect. On the American side, there was nothing but vast confusion, and indecision. Admiral Turner had flown into Guadalcanal on September 11 to deliver some really bad news—his commanding officer, the unfortunate Ghormley, had concluded that he no longer had the resources to support the Marines on Guadalcanal.

Turner wasn't so defeatist, but he had come up with an absolutely absurd strategy to defend the Marine position—an "ink spot" deployment in which small units would be stationed at every possible landing site to oppose Japanese landings. As historian Frank points out, that had one major flaw: the Japanese were already on the island in force.

Fortunately, those of us manning the thinly defended lines had no notion of any of this. And I don't suppose "Red Mike" Edson would have given it much thought even if he had known about it. He had 840 men under his command, Raiders and Parachutists, to defend the ridge.

Edson knew the Japanese were coming, but the word hadn't quite reached everyone else. Over to the east, where Major Ishitari's First Battalion of Oka's 124th Regiment lay waiting concealed in the jungle beside a large, grassy field, the Americans' reconnaissance efforts were laughable. An American patrol, maybe thirty men, stumbled out into the field at noon on the twelfth and became so engrossed in eating their rations and watching the dogfights overhead, they failed to notice more than nine hundred rifles were aimed their way. Major Ishitari resisted temptation; even though he could almost reach out and touch the Americans, he let them go on their happy way. When I read Ishitari's diary, describing this encounter, I blanched, for I was the leader of that happy-go-lucky patrol. Sometimes you don't know who your true friends are. Thank you, Major Ishitari.

Kawaguchi was quietly going mad. He had no idea what Oka was up to; he seemed to be constantly running into troubles of one kind or another, and the result was delay after delay, excuse after excuse. The Kuma Battalion was working its way into position to attack us, but they were having serious troubles locating our lines. Many of Kawaguchi's units south of the ridge had lost their way, too, to the point where poor Kawaguchi was in danger of losing control of the battle.

An enemy plane dropped a flare over the ridge at 9 p.m. on September 12. Half an hour later, a Japanese cruiser and three destroyers opened fire on Marine positions. (Admiral Turner was still meeting with Vandegrift when the shells began whistling overhead. He had doubted the Marines' contention that a major attack was under way. He doubted it no longer, and the next morning he said he would do everything he could to rush reinforcements to the island.)

Minutes later, Kawaguchi managed to push forward the first of his planned attacks, though it was hardly synchronized the way he had intended. Edson's lines swayed under the attack but didn't break. Veterans can still see Edson, sitting on a log eating cold meat and cold potatoes. "Testing, just testing," he said of the Japanese attacks. He predicted they would be back, stronger than before.

To prepare for it, he moved his positions two hundred yards to the rear to give the Japanese a new look. And then he and his Marines waited. The attack began at 6:30 p.m. the next day, the thirteenth. Ishitari and his First Battalion, anchoring the Japanese left, led the charge. Within an hour, Ishitari and 230 of his men had been killed and another 100 wounded. The enemy artillery, the survivors recalled, was unspeakably fierce. In fact, Marine gunners had laid down a barrage just two hundred yards in front of their own advanced positions as the Japanese stormed up the hill. By 11 p.m., historian Frank says, a full battalion of 105mm howitzers was blazing away, taking a terrible toll.

Correspondent Tregaskis heard a forward observer's voice on radio calmly ordering the artillery to "drop it five zero and walk it back and forth across the ridge." It was this massed and accurate artillery fire that again and again wrecked Japanese units.

It was now 2 a.m., and it is not an exaggeration to say the battle for Guadalcanal was on the line. Edson was making his last stand with three hundred men in a horseshoe-shaped line on the knoll. Fearing one of his commanders wasn't up to the job, he coolly relieved him and gave his unit to Captain Harry Torgerson, a warrior; he launched a counterattack against the brave, stubborn Japanese troops and drove them back and then called in artillery to finish them off.

Edson watched it all, just ten or fifteen yards behind the firing line, with bullet holes in his collar and shirt. Historian Frank figures an attack by one more Japanese battalion would have carried the day, and for the Japanese the irony is that they had one (from Oka's 124th Regiment, of course), only it had been so badly mismanaged it never reached the front.

By morning it was over, the ridges littered with Japanese dead and wounded. In midafternoon on the fourteenth, Kawaguchi began his long retreat, and late the next day, the fifteenth, he ordered his survivors to withdraw to the other side of the Matanikau River.

But what about Oka? Kawaguchi had listened in vain for the sound of firing from the west that would have told him of the attack of Colonel Oka and his battalion. But Oka had preferred to keep his unit in the comparable comfort of the Matanikau River rather than hack trails up to the American positions, and that deadly artillery behind them. His staff officers, post-action interviews suggested, secretly suspected that he intended to put off his attack until the main attack had been successful so that the going for him would be that much easier. Whatever his thinking, he decided against making the attack he had been ordered to make on the thirteenth. Late the next afternoon, he launched a feeble assault against a thinly held Marine position. He failed to push it home, and when he encountered resistance, he hustled back to his comfortable post on the Matanikau.

Oka was a pudgy, bombastic little man, full of bravado, and, lucky for our side, he would play the reluctant warrior in future engagements on Guadalcanal. The retreat of Kawaguchi and his men was a nightmare. They marched for days without food or water or serious medical care. Hundreds of them died.

First it had been the stumbling Ichiki. Now the Marines had defeated a better man, Kawaguchi. The Japanese high command was stunned, but they were not prepared to give up.

7

Patrolling

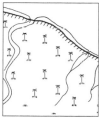 We were well into the Guadalcanal campaign now, and still we had no decent maps.

This didn't deeply concern McKelvy because he couldn't read maps anyway. But he did love a touch of showmanship, and when he discovered that one of our men, Corporal Wike, was a pretty fair draftsman, he decided to have some fun.

He instructed Wike to draw up a battalion map, using all his skills at lettering. It was a handsome affair, completed at night in a tent by the light of an acetylene lamp, full of redundant details. The lettering was especially impressive. "North Coast of Guadalcanal—Lunga Area," it would say. "Third Battalion, First Marines, Lt. Col. William N. McKelvy commanding."

McKelvy loved it and he would drag me along with him on visits to other units, ostensibly to inspect their maps. Our visit to his best pal, Colonel Cresswell, commanding the First Battalion, was a case in point.

"Where are your battalion maps, Charlie?"

"Battalion maps?"

"Charlie, you should have a battalion map like this," at which point he signaled me, the straight man in this performance, to reach into the aluminum container I happened to be carrying and unroll Corporal Wike's work of art.

Creswell and all the others would be suitably impressed. McKelvy, of course, would then stride away, shaking his head in feigned disbelief at the mapmaking ignorance of his fellow battalion commanders.

McKelvy spent hours looking at the maps we collected as the campaign wore on, though most of them were fairly useless. He would brood over the possibilities these maps seemed to suggest to him. It was another rare performance, the great American strategist, making his plans, a foeman worthy of the steel of those Japanese strategists across the river, studying their maps.

In the lull following the battle of Edson's Ridge, we began serious efforts to improve our knowledge of Japanese positions and Japanese morale through sophisticated patrolling beyond our perimeter.

Patrolling heretofore had not been one of our strengths. A few days after we landed, a captured Japanese sailor told us the whereabouts of a number of Japanese soldiers and sailors, and said they might be ready to surrender. Our division intelligence officer, Lieutenant Colonel Frank Goettge, decided he would lead a twenty-five-man patrol to locate this pocket of unhappy Japanese fighting men. He and his party left by boat the night of August 12. The minute they stepped ashore, Goettge was killed by enemy fire—and so was the Japanese sailor. The rest of the patrol, with two or three survivors, was wiped out too.

The Japanese sailor probably told us the truth, as far as he knew it. The fact is, Japanese prisoners—they were enlisted men, rarely officers—were usually in a state of shock, trembling, and sometimes making hand gestures pleading to be killed. One of my jobs was to take the captured soldiers up to division headquarters where they would be interviewed by Major Buckley, a former missionary fluent in Japanese and a true expert. "The war is over for you," he would say. "The lieutenant here tells me you have fought well." That was always well received, having an enormous effect on the prisoner. Major Buckley would continue with soothing words, and soon the prisoner would begin telling us what he knew.

The prisoners were confined to an enclosure near the field hospital. The sign said "Camp Tojo" or something very much like it. The sergeant in charge was a jolly fellow, and he became quite friendly with his guests. He gave his prisoners considerable freedom. I can attest to that. One morning, I was awakened by a touch on the shoulder and found a Japanese soldier staring at me. "My God," I thought to myself, "they've broken through." But, of course, they hadn't; the man was a prisoner and he simply wanted to collect my laundry to be cleaned at the Tojo Laundry.

The prisoners were a sorry lot, and generally we treated them with kindness. Occasionally, though, they were shot, much to the chagrin of those who had hoped to interview them. Invariably, these killings were committed by rear-echelon troops seeking to demonstrate misplaced valor.

Vandegrift became so impatient with what he perceived to be our lack of patrolling skills that he assigned Lieutenant Colonel William J. Whaling, executive officer of the Fifth Marines, to form a special unit of men for scouting and sniping. Most of his men had been hunters in civilian life, and many of them became serious characters in the great Marine Corps tradition.

But I don't recall Whaling's operation having much effect on us. We went ahead with patrolling, learning our lessons along the way. Jungle patrols were damn hard work, as I conveyed in this letter to Dad and Margaret:

When the battles die down, there is ceaseless patrol activity in the jungle—a sort of no-man's land. The terrain is fascinating—steep grass-covered coral ridges, deep ravines you have to climb down hanging onto vines like a monkey to keep from falling. The trees are tremendous—giant Dilo trees as high as 180 feet and banyan and eucalyptus trees almost as large.

You have no idea of how tiring a patrol is. The heat is terrific and because of security measures you're loaded down with ammunition, grenades, emergency rations, machetes, etc. We usually carry two weapons, one of them a Thompson or Reising sub-machine gun.

Trying to get up the slippery banks of the many mountain-fed streams (torrents after a rain and it always rains in the mountains) is the worst part as you have to keep your weapons out of the mud.

Last but not least are our jungle friends—the Nips. You have to watch every clump of bushes for snipers and machine guns. You also have to listen to the birds and distinguish between the real McCoy and the phony bird calls the Japs use.

We ran into a bunch of Japs some time ago. I had a patrol of six and myself. Our mission was to locate the Jap positions as our offensive began at dawn the next day. We spotted one area in front of a 75mm gun a friend of mine had taken the breech block out of earlier (while the Japs slept). His patrol was pumping tommy guns at them, so we swung north and went through the jungle up the beach and went along the ridges to the north, finding two Jap 37mm guns emplaced and camouflaged at a bend in the road. As the gun crew was obligingly sleeping or eating somewhere we tinkered with the guns with the aid of a screwdriver until it would take a mechanical genius to put them back together again (still have a breech block as a souvenir).

We then skirted the coral formations (caves, etc.) along the shore until I spotted what appeared to be a Marine standing up behind a sort of coral "igloo" with a gun port in it about 20 yards away. Then I heard the Jap bird-call signal (one long note, one short) and the Marine turned around and saw me. For a Marine he looked very, very Japanese. I shot at him with my .45, missing him quite completely. I ducked for cover (as my Nipponese was likewise doing) and the rest of the patrol flopped down into firing positions behind logs, trees, etc.

We had evidently surprised the gun crews of the 37mm for they started rushing around for cover by the little coral "igloos." Fortunately all three men on our left had Thompsons and three Japs who tore across for cover were literally torn to shreds. The rest of the Japs started shooting (at what I don't know as their shots came nowhere near us) and jabbering quite excitedly. A couple stuck their heads up to see what was going on. The man on my right got one and I got the other.

Finally all shooting stopped but a machine gun to our left opened up. As we were about three-quarters of a mile away, we knew that an exit would not be injudicious. We threw our grenades and then withdrew one by one, the remaining men increasing their fire to make it sound like we were being reinforced. The Japs on our left must have thought we were a small army as they never bothered us. We must have sounded like one! Six men, three Thompson sub-machine guns, three Reising sub-machine guns, five rifles, three .45 caliber pistols plus a weird assortment of grenades, knives, and wire to fix up booby traps. The men were all ready to go and get the Jap headquarters and were grinning broadly as they pulled out their knives and looked at me as if to ask could they rush in. As later events proved, the place was honeycombed with machine-gun positions so I still believe discretion is the better part of valor!

I didn't mention in my letter home that we did lose one of our men, Private First Class Dix, to enemy fire during our withdrawal.

We had two patrols out that day. The second was led by my old friend from Officers Candidate School, "Ramrod" Taylor. He commanded our battalion's mortar platoon, and for days he and the men in their observation post had been looking in vain for some Japanese 37s that were hurling shells at our position. But all they could see were the white cockatoos endlessly fluttering above the foliage that screened us from the enemy positions.

So Taylor marched into McKelvy's tent and asked permission to take a patrol out there and destroy the guns. It seemed preposterous—the enemy was solidly entrenched on the steep ridges . . . there was undoubtedly a heavy screen of forward observers and snipers, not to mention close infantry support of the gun positions. However, McKelvy, like everyone else, was sick of the shelling too, so at last he gave in to Taylor's request.

Ramrod asked but one thing—twenty-four hours to lay his plans. He was a perfectionist, and he wanted to make this patrol as perfect as he could. He spent the rest of the day with me, the Intelligence officer, minutely examining a recent aerial strip of the territory across the river. Yet even with the use of stereo glasses there was no clue to any enemy activity. Shell holes, native tracks, Melanesian huts, yes—but no telltale blast-flattened grass or fresh trails. With no indications to go on, the two of us could but examine the enemy capabilities, and by making a study of the terrain, list them in order of probability. We even made a mud castle showing what we knew of the Japanese positions on the other side of the river.

Since the shells were high-velocity 37s, all deeply defiladed (meaning deeply sloped) places could be eliminated. We were looking for spots with moderate defilade and covered ravines leading to them for supply routes. We finally picked five locations that seemed to fulfill our requirements, and numbered them on the photos. It was now midafternoon, time for the Japanese gunners to begin throwing their usual four o'clock salvos at the ridges. By listening carefully to this gunfire, we were able to eliminate two of our locations as being too far south.

So now we had three possible locations. We then determined a route that would allow Taylor to pierce the enemy screen of observers and snipers, bypass strong points, and reach our target locations under cover. We also figured out a primary and alternate route to get the hell out of there if things went wrong.

We set out at the same time (I described the results for my patrol in my letter home). Taylor and his little group of volunteers—everybody wanted to go with Taylor—cautiously paddled across the river in a rubber boat just at dawn, silently alighted on the west bank, and crept slowly through the dense canebreak. Wordlessly, the men followed in file behind Taylor as he skirted along the wooden slopes of a ravine he knew would lead him near Location No. 1. At length he reached it, took out his aerial photograph, checked it to make sure of just where he was, and then sent his first scout forward to reconnoiter the spot.

The scout crawled slowly up a little gully until he had come almost to the top, but looking around he saw no gun—only a pile of dried grass. It was then that a small breeze stirred and he caught the sickly muskish odor of sweat and Japanese perfume. Crawling up the grass pile, he brushed some grass away—and stared straight into the muzzle of a Jap 37.

He summoned the rest of the patrol, and they came forward immediately. It was at that crucial moment they heard the sharp barking of a dog. To their horror, Taylor and his men peered down into a ravine and saw that the barking was coming from a mean-looking cur who was frantically trying to awaken his Japanese masters peacefully sleeping in their bivouac at the bottom of the ravine.

Determined to profit from this display of typical Japanese overconfidence, Taylor told his men to sit tight at Location No. 1 while he lone-wolfed it to Location No. 2. Arriving there he was greeted with the sight of another 37, visible at close range through its camouflage. As he approached the gun, Ramrod looked down into the ravine at a group of native huts and saw four Japanese soldiers watching his every move. Taylor hesitated a moment, and then waved at them cordially. Just as cordially, the Japanese waved back. As they lazily watched him, Taylor calmly removed the vital parts of the gun's breech block, stemming his instinctive desire to shoot and run. The gun dismantled, he waved again to his new friends and walked back slowly along the ridge, hunching over to make himself as diminutive as possible.

Reunited with his men, he tarried only long enough to leave a calling card—a message of greeting—in the gun barrel. He and his men followed the main withdrawal route and reentered our lines, mission accomplished.

Two days later, McKelvy asked that we repeat our patrols, with Taylor following the same route. This was an incredibly stupid mistake, very much like the decision to send the light tanks back on the same path they had used before. That led to disaster, and so would this.

We pushed off before dawn, again by rubber boat. Ramrod's group turned left and began climbing the steep ridge. I turned right with my patrol, heading on a different route for Point Cruz. Ramrod and I had agreed there was a strong chance that there were some high-ranking Japanese officers there. Capturing them would be a great coup.

Eventually we came upon a sudden opening in the thicket, and there, just in front of us, stood a dozen Japanese soldiers. They had been cooking something over a fire, and they were as surprised to see us as we were surprised to see them. We had the drop on them, and opened up with everything we had. Both sides fired; both sides missed.

My men were all for rushing forward to capture or kill these soldiers. Instead, we opted for discretion, moving across the sandbar to the safety of our own positions. I was taken to see "Red Mike" Edson, now a colonel and commanding officer of the Fifth Marines, readying his men for an attack. I told him what I had seen and emphasized the dangers of his Point Cruz position.

"Thank you," Edson said. "You've had a hard day, lieutenant, so why not relax a little and let me carry on and run the regiment." It was about then I shuddered. You never can help shuddering, just a little, when you've done something like this. I had volunteered, and I was lucky.

Not so Ramrod. When we were fighting our way out of Point Cruz, we thought we heard some whistling noises, maybe signals from Taylor. They were shots, and some of them must have killed my friend.

We learned later that the Japanese had been waiting for Taylor's patrol at Location No. 1. When they attacked, Taylor turned to his men and told them to run for the river while he held off the Japanese. They refused. He ordered them to leave. Reluctantly, they left him and headed for home. From the sound of the heavy firing it was obvious Taylor was preventing the Japanese from making any kind of pursuit. About the time his men reached our lines, the firing stopped. It meant one thing—Taylor was dead.

We mourned his loss. We berated our complicity in going along with McKelvy's insistence of retracing the route of Taylor's first patrol. In the end, we insisted that McKelvy put Ramrod in for a Navy Cross. He didn't want to—he never sought recognition for any of his men—but this time we refused to back down. Ramrod Taylor won a Navy Cross (and so, when the battle was over and we were headed home, did Bill McKelvy).

Through these combat patrols (and the interviews with prisoners captured during them) we began to compile some very helpful information about our enemy. Colonel Cates, our regimental commander, put a lot of it together in an intelligence report dated September 6.

Japanese officers, he said, "all carried sabers and automatic pistols of various makes, ranging in caliber from .25 to .38. The Nambu automatic pistol (model 1925), cal. 7mm, was found on several officers. The 8mm cal. of the same make was carried by many of the non-commissioned officers.

"The individual soldier," the colonel wrote, "carried two types of rifle—one, the Arushe, cal. .256 (model 1905) and the other, the cal. 7.7mm (model 1919) of the same make. Bayonets are carried by every soldier and are very sharp, and with a hooked ring to catch opponent's blade. In hand to hand fighting, it was noted they held their bayonets in their hands and used them as swords. They all carried hand grenades and used them frequently, but they had a very small bursting radius.

"The Nambu light machine gun (cal. 7.7mm) was an effective weapon, and they used light and portable grenade throwers (model 1899) to considerable advantage.

"In general," Cates said, "the Japanese equipment is far inferior to ours in every respect. With the exception of their 7.7mm machine gun— the Nambu—their weapons look like our 1898 vintage." Cates might have added that the Marines landed on Guadalcanal still carrying the old bolt-action 1903 Springfield rifle, itself a pretty good carry-back to 1898 vintage. When the Army troops relieved us, they carried the new semi-automatic M-1s, giving them, on paper at least, a lot more firepower. Our Reising submachine gun was a loser too. It was a flimsy weapon, constantly jamming and breaking down. It was popularly called the "Rusting gun" by those of us who carried it. We gave up on it early on, and thereafter trusted the old Thompson submachine gun to balance things out.

"The pack carried by individual Japanese soldiers was always scrupulously clean," Cates wrote. "We found it contained camouflage nets for helmets and shoulders with twigs and grass woven into them; a three-piece set of cooking utensils; two or three cans of food, sweet cakes, bread and rice; an extra pair of shoes, either sneakers or hobnails, underclothes, socks, and toilet articles.

"Almost every soldier kept a diary, something we don't allow on our side. Sometimes, we found, they carried opium. In some of the packs were small Japanese flags with writing scrawled on them. Each soldier carried a first-aid kit containing two sterile triangular bandages and two picrid acid gauzes for burns.

"Officers and non-commissioned officers carried heavy leather dispatch cases, with notebooks, and crude maps.

"Their tactics," Cates reported, "were puzzling. In the first fight, the battle of the Tenaru, the Japanese relied on the surprise of a quick night assault in large numbers and supporting fire from heavy and light machine guns and those portable grenade throwers. Rather than keeping low to the sandspit, which closes the mouth of the Tenaru, they charged standing straight up with small intervals between them. On receiving our fire, they continued to expose themselves with utter disregard for life. Those who were able to reach this side of the river were in great confusion and for the most part leaderless. The officers, who led the advance across the sandbar, were the first to be shot.

"They showed a tendency to bunch up, so that sometimes three or four machine guns were placed so close together they were within bursting range of one of our heavy mortar shells. Five men were seen taking cover around the same tree.

"They were experts at camouflage, but their marksmanship was poor.

"Reduced to desperate conditions, many Japanese lay among their own casualties, played dead, and when Marines drew near rose up to throw hand grenades at them. Suicides were numerous when capture became evident. During hand to hand combat, the Japanese emitted wild yells and brandished their weapons fiercely."

Cates noted something we had found again and again—the fact that the Japanese, close up, had what we found to be a distinctive odor. "You can actually smell a Jap at a good distance," is the way Cates put it (it is possible, I suppose, that they could smell us, too). "They use some kind of powder which permeates the atmosphere and our men on the front lines can sometimes tell when they are near. The odor is a sweet sickening one, but it is perfume compared to a dead Jap after a few hours exposure to the hot sun. The smell, two days after the battle of the Tenaru, made a lot of us lose our lunches."

I took a stab at examining Japanese fighting skills, with some criticism of our own performance, after one of my patrols, and I put it down in writing (a copy of which is reproduced in Cates's unpublished manuscript).

GENERAL ESTIMATE:

1. Most noticeable fact was—amazing lack of precautions taken for security. Patrols got within 15–20 yards of enemy groups and

opened fire first. Enemy propensity for leaving guns unattended inexplicable. Either morale at such a state they don't give a damn, or else on basis of previous experience in Java and Malaya totally unprepared for enemy patrol activity. Evidently expected us to remain behind our barbed wire defenses as had previous opponents.

Terrain ideal for use of large vine-covered trees as CPs. High ground to south of beach has plenty of high knolls and ridges commanding all approaches to bivouac areas and gun positions. (Enemy does use bird-call warning system—one long, one short—to signal enemy approaching but does not exploit it fully.)

2. Enemy tactics: Terrain superb for long-range sniping. High ground descending steeply to river in vicinity of bend offers covered positions with FULL VIEW OF OUR LINES AND ACTIVITY BEHIND OUR LINES. Sniping could be done at range of 150–1,000 yards with an abundance of lucrative Marine targets always in sight. Yet, despite the fact the enemy was bivouaced in this area, there is no evidence of any sniping. Rather they evidently kept close to the caves they had constructed in the sides of the ravines.

NOTE: Observing from enemy territory, our camouflage and camouflage discipline is almost non-existent. Enough activity and noise could be observed of our lines and of the ridges behind to keep a dozen enemy CPs snowed under sending dope in. If bush hides our bivouac areas, enough yelling and shouting is furnished to give away the position. Sand-bag emplacements were very easy to spot and a continual flow of traffic over the ridges was always in evidence. Jeep drivers' racing of motors accurately designated the course of our roads. On the other hand, all enemy positions . . . were skillfully camouflaged with leaves and branches. However, the enemy nullifies the camouflage effect to a great extent by engaging in loud and excited jabbering back and forth when under fire.

3. Enemy morale: Low. Members of outposts probably physically weak and suffering from hunger, and probably very unhappy about the whole thing. They made no effort to retrieve their dead comrades lying within 200 yards of them, nor did they take advantage of their excellent observation at the mouth of the Matanikau River to harass us with sniping.

We all believed we were beginning to win this crucial battle, but we still had a long way to go, and our turn was soon to come.

8

Our Turn

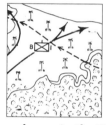 The great conundrum about the Third Battalion, First Marines, on Guadalcanal was simple enough: Why did we fight so effectively for such an eccentric commanding officer? He drank too much. He was terrified of being criticized by his superiors. He was mean to his staff, all of whom served him well. He begrudged support for his men. His battalion was the only one in the First Marines that failed to win its share of decorations. Yet, when it counted, we came through for him.

I go back to the day McKelvy called me into his makeshift command post and said he had an important job for me: collect a supply of white tape, in anticipation of possible trouble. The tape was to mark a retreat trail in the event our forward positions were overwhelmed.

As I was preparing to mark a line of retreat, McKelvy was touring our various strong points to jolly things up. At one stop, I was told later, an officer commanding a 75mm gun on a half-track asked McKelvy what he and his men should do in the event the Japanese overran his position. Should they retreat?

"Retreat?" McKelvy bellowed. He seemed stupefied at the very notion. "Jesus wept! The only man to retreat will be dragging the gun's breech block on his bloody stumps!"

The men smiled, jabbing each other at the sheer bravado of the old man's performance. They loved this kind of talk, and McKelvy was a master at it. Never mind that I was collecting the tape to mark the very line of retreat he said he would never contemplate.

That was one of his secrets—he couldn't fool the officers, who saw so much more of him, but he knew how to play to the troops.

None of us who served with this extraordinary character will ever forget the day in early October he volunteered our unit to make what was supposed to be a feint—a fake—landing at Kokumbona, where we all suspected the Japanese were strongly entrenched.

The real attack was to come from the west, carried out by elements from the Fifth and the newly arrived Seventh Marines. We were supposed to divert the Japanese by pretending to storm the beaches at Kokumbona. None of us was very happy about undertaking this assignment. We had seen more than our share of fighting in the preceding weeks, and there was a general feeling among the officers that McKelvy was volunteering us for the job so he could grab some glory for himself.

The colonel had been chafing for some time about the lack of a plan that would get the Third Battalion into dramatic action. This was hardly that kind of plan, but maybe it could be. What if McKelvy could notify division headquarters that the coast was clear at Kokumbona, so that we could make a full-scale attack? We guessed what McKelvy was thinking— we were experts at that by now—and we worried that he would make the landing, whether the Japanese were there or not.

The men were happily unaware of any of the suspicions of their officers, and we saw no reason to spread our concerns. As the men talked over the forthcoming assault, their resolve hardened. I remember Captain Putnam, head of I Company, giving a particularly rousing assessment of the situation to his troops. "Goddamit," he declared, "we're the Third Battalion of the First Marines!" McKelvy listened with silent approval. Here at last, he must have figured, was his battalion's big moment.

So, on October 8, we began the attack—eight hundred men heading for Kokumbona in Higgins boats arranged in a line abreast. A lone destroyer guarded our flanks. The idea was we would look fearsome enough to hold the Japanese main force from moving to defend against the attack being launched by the Fifth Marines for thirty minutes.

As we rounded the bend at Point Cruz, our destroyer began laying down a fierce barrage from its 5-inch guns. We moved closer and closer, finally turning to full speed for the run-in to the beach. Everything was going as planned, except that we were now getting dangerously close to the Japanese guns we were sure were waiting for us.

McKelvy was in his element. Onward his brave eight hundred sped. His officers weren't so happy. We began looking at each other, in some trepidation. Finally a shot rang out—most likely from a Japanese 37mm gun. It was our deliverance. "The son of a bitch is shooting at us!" the colonel declared, as water from the exploding shell drenched the men aboard his Higgins boat. "Let's get the hell out of here!" And so we turned around and headed back to the safety of our own lines. We all breathed a sigh of relief.

That feint attack McKelvy had volunteered us for was a part of a series of offensive operations that began along the Matanikau on September 23 and went from bad to better. In the first phase, the First Battalion, Seventh Marines, and the First Raider Battalion set out on a reconnaissance in force in the area between Mt. Austen and Kokumbona.

The Seventh Marines, the Corps' all-star regiment that had been separated and sent off to defend Samoa, arrived on Guadalcanal on September 14. The regiment's First Battalion was commanded by Lieutenant Colonel Lewis B. "Chesty" Puller, already a legend in the Marine Corps. Puller with his fresh nine-hundred-man battalion began the attack on September 23 and ran into trouble the next day. Puller was reinforced by troops from the Fifth Marines, and then all of them ran into more trouble. Even the ineffable Colonel Oka staged a stout resistance with his Twelfth Company on the east bank of the Matanikau River, near the One Log Bridge. Vandegrift was forced to dispatch the First Raider Battalion to lend a hand. Edson, now in command of all the attacking troops, finally called the whole thing off, and the Marines straggled home. They had lost sixty killed and a hundred wounded.

"It taught me a great lesson—the danger of overconfidence," Vandegrift wrote in his memoirs. "Obviously the Matanikau area held a far stronger enemy than I had suspected. I still wanted to move against him, and I would. But next time I would move more slowly and in much greater strength."

Vandegrift and his key commanders continued to curse the Navy, and especially Admiral Kelly Turner, whose latest brainstorm involved a proposal to send the Second Raider Battalion off on a wild goose chase against a number of insignificant Japanese outposts. Vandegrift wanted Carlson's Second Raiders in relief of Edson's First Raiders, who had by now seen about as much action as any unit could handle.

He was able to tell his side of the story to the top admiral himself, Chester Nimitz, when he flew in to muddy Henderson Field on the last day of September aboard an Army Air Corps B-17. Vandegrift told Nimitz that Turner's idea was ludicrous and added that one of the Navy's big problems was that its skippers worried too much about running their ships aground. The main mission for the Marines on Guadalcanal, now and always, he told the admiral, was holding Henderson Field. Nimitz, Vandegrift concluded, got the message. He was "a very perceptive officer who recognized logic when he saw it."

Nimitz's day on Guadalcanal damn near ended with his death when the B-17 trying to take off on the muddy runway failed to reach speed, and the pilot had to shut down his engines and hit the brakes. "The bomber slithered maddeningly along, stopping finally with its nose hanging over the edge of the field not far from the trees." Nimitz and the B-17 got away safely later, when the field had dried out a little.

The Japanese, meanwhile, were slipping reinforcements through to Guadalcanal, including some big howitzers they hoped to use to pound Henderson Field.

October was going to decide the fate of Guadalcanal, and I think we all realized the key point might be the sandspit at the mouth of the Matanikau River. Why so important? Well, the river was narrow and the ridges and banks were so precipitous that it wasn't fordable. The one spot at which heavy equipment could be transported from one side of the river to the other was this sandspit running across the mouth. Since the big drive now being planned by the Japanese depended so much on moving tanks and heavy artillery from the west side of the river to the east side, Lieutenant General Masao Maruyama, commander of the newly arrived Second "Sendai" Division, was ordered to secure a strong position on the east bank. This was an elite division in the Japanese army, founded many years earlier by the Emperor Shintake, its men recruited from the Sendai district of Honshu. It had served earlier in Manchuria and had taken part in the invasion of Java.

Maruyama, in constant pain from attacks of neuralgia, had arrived on Guadalcanal himself on October 3. The pain intensified when he was told that of the nine thousand Japanese troops landed earlier on Guadalcanal (not counting his troops from the Second Division), two thousand were now dead, and five thousand more were in no condition for sustained combat operations. By October 5, however, Maruyama had succeeded in deploying two battalions and parts of a third on the east side of the river, across the sandspit.

These reinforcements had no idea things were so bad on Guadalcanal. They had been told before making the landing that the campaign was progressing on schedule. But here they met the shattered remnants of Kawaguchi's brigade who told them these Marines weren't the luxury-loving cowards everyone presumed them to be; instead, the campaign veterans said, these Marines were fierce, brutal murderers, scraped from the scum of prisons and insane asylums in the United States.

These brutal Marines were heading for the sandspit, too, in the second phase of the offensive operation that had begun late in September. This time, Vandegrift, with a lot more care and caution, committed five infantry battalions from the Fifth and Seventh Marines and Colonel Whaling's exotic sniper-scout unit. On October 7, Marine historian John Zimmerman wrote, the Third Battalion, Fifth Marines, made contact with a small force of Japanese just east of the Matanikau. With the Japanese giving way slowly, Edson called in reinforcements, including the weary survivors in his old Raider Battalion. It rained hard part of the day on the eighth—the day McKelvy led us on that feint landing against Kokumbona—but by late afternoon Whaling's sniper-scouts and the Seventh Marines were in position, and the Japanese still on the east bank of the Matanikau were perilously close to being cut off from their main body.

The ring closed the next day—October 9—and all of the Japanese troops were cleared from the east bank of the Matanikau at the sandspit and the position secured by Marines. It was a substantial victory for us, followed up two days later by a substantial victory by the Navy, in the Battle of Cape Esperance, when the Japanese lost four ships and six hundred men in a night action.

Yet, just two days later, Japanese ships were back, on a night that is forever remembered by Marine veterans of Guadalcanal as "The Bombardment." In a terrifying episode never to be repeated in World War II, two Japanese battleships, *Kongo* and *Haruna,* opened fire on Marine positions with their giant 12-inch and 14-inch guns. A Japanese observation plane—they were all called "Louie the Louse"—had flown over Henderson Field in advance of the bombardment and dropped flares.

It was an incredibly harrowing experience. These giant battleships were close inshore, and the sound those guns made was one of doom. The attack was illuminated by recurrent lightning-like flashes that bounced off the mountain range several miles to the south. The people in charge at the field hospital had dug a long trench and covered it with tin and wood. This elaborate trench, it turned out, offered the worst possible protection against these big shells. The men were crowded together in the trench, instead of being dispersed in individual foxholes. The blasts from the shells traveled the length of the trench, causing concussions. Some of the men simply went mad.

You could actually hear the shells rumbling through the air as they approached our positions. Seconds later, there would be a great thunderclap as the shells dug into the fetid soil and then exploded. One of them killed Pete Richards, an old friend from my days at St. Andrew's School.

The bombardment rained down on us the same day as our first Army reinforcements, the 164th Infantry Regiment, a National Guard outfit from North Dakota, arrived on the island. Professionals often joke about the shortcomings of Guard units, but this one, commanded by a West Pointer, Lieutenant Colonel Bryant E. Moore, was special. Moore is remembered by Guadalcanal veterans as the officer who ordered one of his own company commanders to switch jobs, and rank, with his first sergeant.

The Japanese were firing a special Type 3 shell, historian Richard Frank reported, designed for anti-aircraft work but just as devastating when fired at aircraft on the ground. The first rounds struck west of the airfield, but in no time at all the shells were hitting their targets with extraordinary accuracy, destroying American planes and ammunition and fuel dumps.

The Japanese battleships broke off the attack about 2:15 the morning of October 14, their commanders worried about pesky American PT boats that had been shooting off torpedoes—most of which didn't work—in their direction.

The battleships had fired 973 shells and destroyed all but seven of the planes tied down for the night at Henderson Field. Gone up in flames, too, was all the aviation fuel. Planes tied up at the shorter fighter strip fared a little better; half of them survived.

Vandegrift reported that the situation was now so desperate that Major Jack Cram, the pilot of a lumbering old PBY, strapped two torpedoes under the seaplane's wings and took off to challenge enemy ships, now swarming around the island. He may even have hit one.

"The enemy was hurting us and he knew it," Vandegrift wrote. He sent a priority dispatch to Nimitz, Ghormley, and Turner, pleading for the

Navy to seize control of the seas surrounding Guadalcanal and urgently requesting reinforcement of his ground forces by at least one division.

On October 18, Nimitz fired poor Ghormley and promoted William F. "Bull" Halsey, a fighting admiral, to take his place. "Jesus Christ and General Jackson! This is the hottest potato they ever handed me," said Halsey as he read his orders. Straight off, he announced that from now on naval officers in his area of operations—the South Pacific—no longer had to wear neckties. Hours later, he sent this order to one of his admirals: "Strike, repeat, strike." The next day in Washington, Navy Secretary Frank Knox was asked at his press conference if the Marines on Guadalcanal could hold. "I certainly hope so," he replied.

On Guadalcanal, weary Marines began singing a parody of the British Army song, "Bless 'em All." It went this way, division historian George McMillan recalled.

Oh we asked for the Army to come to Tulagi,
  But Douglas MacArthur said, No!
He gave as his reason,
  This isn't the season,
Besides, there is no U.S.O.

For we're saying goodbye to them all
  As back to our foxholes we crawl!
There'll be no promotion
  This side of the ocean
So cheer up, my lads.
  Bless 'em all.

On the Japanese side, the situation on Guadalcanal was now critical. And there to share in it—he landed on the island on October 10—was Lieutenant General Harukichi Hyakutake, commander of the Imperial Seventeenth Army, taking personal command.

While the Americans desperately flew in fifty-five-gallon drums of airplane fuel aboard cargo planes and drained gasoline from wrecked planes cleared from the hastily repaired runway, the Japanese high-speed convoys brought reinforcements and supplies to their beleaguered troops on the island.

Part of the new offensive was a propaganda campaign, chiefly radio shows aimed at the Marines defending Guadalcanal. Some of it was pretty clever, particularly the "Zero Hour," with an English-speaking woman who called herself Little Orphan Annie reminding us of the hopelessness of our position and hinting at the faithlessness of our wives and sweethearts back home. With Little Orphan Annie, bombers, artillery, and battleships, the softening up that would lead to the climactic battle was well under way.

Hyakutake deeply regretted the loss of the beachhead on the eastern bank of the Matanikau, and worried if he could win it back. The problem was not so much lack of artillery to sustain such an attack, it was the shortage of ammunition. Hyakutake leaned heavily on his Second Division operations officer, Lieutenant Colonel Hiroshi Matsumoto, for estimates of enemy strength and for proposals on how to defeat him. On October 11, Matsumoto and several other Japanese officers climbed up Mt. Austen to a position called Mambulo where they could virtually look down the throats of the Americans. The Americans couldn't move a truck, a plane, or a Higgins boat without it being spotted through the powerful Japanese telescopes. It was true we had become somewhat more skillful in camouflaging the movement of our patrols, but there were few larger troop movements that weren't tracked daily by the Japanese lookouts.

Matsumoto, after peering through one of those big telescopes, became convinced that the Americans were not seriously defending their positions south of the airfield. He and his fellow officers also became convinced that the land south of the airport wasn't as rugged as they had thought (though this surely was the lesson learned by Kawaguchi's Japanese troops who had attempted to penetrate it earlier in the campaign). Historian Frank also noted a delicious irony—the Japanese had bigger problems with maps than we did. They were using the same useless charts of the Mt. Austen area we had been using (and that had caused such a sharp exchange between me and McKelvy). These charts showed gently sloping terrain that looked as if it could be easily traversed. At least we came to recognize that the lines on the charts were merely decorative; the Japanese at this late date continued to believe they were meaningful.

And so Hyakutake changed his attack plan to include still another surprise attack from the south, over the same ground that had taken Kawaguchi to disaster in September. This attack would be led by General Maruyama, with nine infantry battalions from the fresh Sendai Division.

After the early fighting, Vandegrift had with considerable tact relieved some of his officers, including battalion commanders, who had failed to perform up to expectations, and replaced them with more aggressive, and usually younger, officers. The Japanese had done nothing about their failures, and now the greatest failure of all, the Marines' best friend, Colonel Oka, returned to the fray.

Oka was ordered to take his 124th Regiment, with elements of the Fourth Infantry Regiment, to the west bank of the Matanikau and cross to the east side at the One Log Bridge, and then launch his attack on the Marines defending the east bank of the river at the sandspit from the south. At the same time, Colonel Nakaguma and most of the troops from his Fourth Regiment, led by the First Independent Tank Company, would force a crossing of the sandspit, west to east, where we—McKelvy's Third Battalion—were dug in.

Like Oka, Kawaguchi should have been relieved by now, but he was still taking a leading role in the surprise attack that Hyakutake was launching from the jungle south of the airport. And he didn't like any part of it. He complained so much that he was dismissed from his post, and command supposedly fell to Colonel Shoji of the 230th Infantry Regiment. Shoji, though, was feeling poorly and didn't want the job either. Kawaguchi lingered at his post.

Maruyama, in command of the southern front, had hoped to begin his surprise attack on October 22. But, hardly any surprise, his troops had become bogged down, and sometimes hopelessly lost, in the steamy jungles. Came the twenty-third and the force was still out of position, and so Maruyama had to postpone H-hour again, this time until 5 p.m. on the twenty-fourth.

The biggest problem for both of these armies, slugging away in these jungles, was disease. In a monograph called "Jap Medical Problems in the South and Southwest Pacific," published by Navy and Marine specialists on Christmas Day in 1944, the anonymous authors noted that Guadalcanal was "extraordinary in that, of all the major campaigns in the Pacific theater, this one was without doubt affected most markedly by medical factors. Though both sides suffered severely, the Japanese suffered the most. . . . In view of the closeness of the decision in some of the engagements, the narrow margin by which enemy capture of the airfield was averted, and the near-success of some of the major enemy land attacks, it might well be that had the enemy been able to keep his forces up to strength and in good physical condition, the narrow margin of failure would have been converted into success," the report concluded.

Our troops began coming down with malaria in September, and by November about 15 percent of all our troops on the island were infected. I picked up malaria myself and spent months following the campaign in rehabilitation; I had recurring attacks for years after the battle had ended.

We didn't do as much as we could; the program to force our troops to take Atabrine and quinine medication was never properly enforced. What made it worse was the rumor that taking Atabrine cut down on a man's sexual powers. Still, we were able to take our sick to an under-staffed field hospital, where they were given adequate rest and treat-ment. The Japanese had nothing of the kind. Most Japanese suffering from malaria, the authors of the medical report stated, "were made to stay in the lines and fight because of their great need for troops. Turning in for treatment was discouraged, and many died of malaria in foxholes in the line. . . . The sick who were treated were ordinarily laid out on mats or on the ground in the jungle and sometimes given some scant shelter by means of palm thatch. Sanitation in these out-door sick bays was atrocious. The sick were reluctant to use trench latrines, particularly at night, and deposited their excrement in the immediate vicinity of their mats, whence it was often washed into the lean-to shelters by the rain." Supplies were so short that sometimes sick Japanese soldiers were given intravenous injections of coconut milk, because of the lack of saline solution. Food was extremely short, and coconuts, grass, taro, wild potatoes, fern and bamboo sprouts, and even crocodiles and lizards were used as emergency sources of nourishment.

Guadalcanal was a tough campaign for us; it was truly hell for the Japanese.

"In our opinion," the authors of the report stated, "fully two-thirds of the Japanese who met their demise on Guadalcanal died of disease. . . . Thus, of the 42,000 Japanese believed to have faced us on Guadalcanal [the estimate is high], less than one-quarter were killed in action or died of wounds." It may have been the fact that so many of these Japanese troops were riddled with disease that tipped the scales in our favor dur-ing the critical fighting that was now beginning along the Matanikau and in the jungles south of the airfield.

But, malaria or no, the Japanese were heading our way again in what would be their most ambitious offensive operation in the entire cam-paign. They hit my outfit first.

As the sun slowly went down the night of October 22, Colonel Nakaguma's men crawled through the trenches they had dug right up to the banks of the Matanikau, and put their machine guns in position. Anti-tank and 70mm gun crews wheeled their pieces up to camouflaged spots. Not a sound was made, for while more than two thousand men were creeping through the coconut grove to the river, on the other side we were blissfully chatting and smoking next to our foxholes. By the time the sun set, the entire Japanese force was ready to pounce, the tanks within a hundred yards of the spot over which they would race to break through our horseshoe-shaped position.

Suddenly, a red parachute flare went off and the artillery bombardment began. "It looks like this is the night," Lieutenant Colonel Twining, the division's operations officer, noted. Machine guns, grenade dischargers, anti-tank, and 70mm guns joined in with the heavy artillery. The tanks moved to their jump-off positions, the noise of their motors drowned out by the explosion of the shells.

Intelligence officers don't have particular roles to play when their units are under attack. I remember hearing the clanking noises of the Japanese tanks as they moved toward the sandspit, and I moved to a vantage point halfway along the embankment to watch the action. I couldn't really tell how many Japanese were involved, but it seemed to me there were at least five hundred of them.

I saw the lead tank, a fifteen-ton Type 97, with the brave Captain Maeda in command, lumber out into the sandspit, turn, and with the throttle wide open, race toward our positions on the east bank of the river. In the light of our flares, we could see it tear right through the barbed-wire entanglements. With the other tanks roaring into position behind him, Maeda quickly wheeled his tank to the left and raced down our flank, not far from Private Joseph D. R. Champagne's foxhole. Champagne reached out and dropped a hand grenade in one of the tank's tracks. When it exploded, damaging the track, the tank swerved out of control. No sooner had Captain Maeda got it going again when one of our half-tracks, partly concealed in the jungle, opened up with its 75mm gun. Maeda swung his tank into the surf, avoiding the first shot, but the second one got him.

Several jubilant Marines—members of my old platoon, it turned out— grabbed me and dragged me down the bank to see the carnage. It was very grisly, with dead Japanese all over the bottom of the sandspit; some of them had been dragged under by quicksand, so only their heads were visible.

Three Marine "Stuart" tanks suddenly appeared and began cruising back and forth. Soon the ground was covered with gore and intestines. The stench was terrible; so were the flies (to be replaced later by maggots).

The rest of the Japanese tanks never made it across the sandspit; they were all destroyed by anti-tank fire, turning into blazing wrecks. As the crews, screaming in agony from their burns, crawled out of their turrets to escape, we ripped them with machine guns. Of the forty-five tank crewmen taking part in the attack—the only tank attack by the Japanese in the campaign—twenty-eight died, and of the seventeen survivors, seven were badly wounded.

But it wasn't over yet. Behind the blazing tanks came the Banzai-screaming infantry, and it was at this point that the power of massed American artillery fire was most vividly demonstrated. Much of the credit for our success in the Guadalcanal campaign can be attributed to Brigadier General Pedro del Valle, commanding officer of the Eleventh Marines, the artillery regiment. When Nakaguma launched his attack on our position, del Valle faced a tough question—should he move his guns to thwart that attack, or should he keep them where they were to repel the attack he knew was heading our way from the jungles in the south? Fortunately for us, he decided to move the guns our way.

And so, as the Japanese began their infantry attack, forty big howitzers opened up, shooting off six thousand rounds before they were finished. The range in this area was known to the artillerymen, and the areas had been divided into strips parallel to the line of fire from our batteries, Marine historian Zimmerman wrote. "Each battery was assigned one strip, which it could cover merely by increasing or decreasing ('laddering') its range. The estimate of the situation proved to be correct, and the result was the scientific extermination of an enemy force."

Nakaguma's men were caught "like rats in a trap," Colonel Cates wrote in his memoirs.

Still, some of these brave Japanese soldiers kept the fight going—it went on for eight hours before the shooting died—and several of them fashioned little camouflaged rafts of twigs and leaves, slipping down through the marsh weeds and swimming slowly across the river. They were all killed by rifle fire before they even reached midstream.

I wrote my father and stepmother after the battle was over, boasting a little about our prowess (and why not? this was a tremendous defeat for the Japanese). "The whole Jap force," I said, "hit on a narrow front—about one of our platoon's lines. And that's all the further they got too.

All of the tanks were demolished and the Jap infantry about wiped out."

One of the anomalies about our battle at the sandspit was that it wasn't observed by any of the famous war correspondents who had chronicled the campaign—Tregaskis had gone home, and the *New York Times*'s Hanson Baldwin, whose work I admired, hadn't stayed long enough to see the showdown. (In my letter home, I had a bone to pick with Baldwin: "Hanson Baldwin may think they [the Japanese] are terrific jungle fighters, but personally I don't think our boys do badly.")

The fighting flared up again at daybreak on the twenty-fourth, when several hundred Japanese troops attempted to outflank a battalion of the Seventh Marines, defending a position to our left. They were torn to pieces by more massed artillery fire, and when they took refuge in some deep ravines they were attacked by our dive-bombers, which dropped 100-pound fragmentation bombs.

It is still hard to believe, but in this furious battle our battalion, which bore the brunt of it, lost only two men killed and eleven wounded. "It seems like a miracle not to lose more," Colonel Cates wrote.

What amazed all of us was how similar this attack was to the earlier one on the Tenaru (except for the addition this time of tanks). "Evidently," Cates said, "the Japs have never heard of Plutarch's wise words—'In war time it is not permitted to make the same mistake twice.'" All Cates could figure was that they must have thought they could force the point with those highly vulnerable tanks. "Again, they made a serious mistake and underestimated the fighting ability of the First Marines." Cates then went on to repeat his earlier conclusion: "I still claim they are dumb."

But there was one additional factor here that shouldn't be overlooked. Nakaguma should have been supported by an attack against our lines from the south—from those troops led by the egregious Colonel Oka. Where had he been all this time?

He was supposed to have attacked the ridge forming our southern flank early the afternoon of the twenty-third, *before* Nakaguma began his attack across the sandspit. But Major General Ito, his immediate superior, scanned the ridge all day without seeing any evidence that Oka was beginning an attack. As H-hour for Nakaguma's Fourth Regiment drew near, Ito frantically radioed Oka to get a move on. Oka replied with the usual evasions. The result was that all during that awful night, when Nakaguma's unit was destroyed, there was silence on the Marines' southern flank.

Oka later would defend his tardiness by saying he and his troops had become bogged down in difficult terrain, and in fact on the twenty-second he managed to move forward less than half a mile. It wasn't until the twenty-fifth that he entered the battle, attacking the Second Battalion, Seventh Marines, strung out on a saddle ridge south of our position. Mortar fire rained down on Oka, and by the time the fighting was over he had lost three hundred of his men. Oka himself hastily abandoned his command post and trotted back to the safety of the One Log Bridge (sometimes also called the Nippon Bridge).

The Japanese had always intended that the main attack should come, once again, from the jungles to the south of Henderson Field. Captain Oda—not to be confused with Colonel Oka—and his engineers had gone ahead to blaze a trail through the jungle, but the maps were useless. Instead of gently rolling hills, they were working through a series of sharp cliffs and ravines. An argument broke out between Oda and First Lieutenant Hisatomi, one insisting the route was south, the other swearing it was southeast. They finally reached their destination, the Lunga River, on October 17.

Back at Kokumbona, Maruyama was under the impression that everything was moving right on schedule, principally because of engineer Oda's cheery messages. Accordingly, he ordered his main force to advance over Oda's trail, now named Maruyama Road, carrying five days' rations.

Until they reached the headwaters of the Matanikau, the main body made fairly good progress, but when the soldiers got to those towering cliffs the trouble began. Oda's lightly equipped trailblazers had been able to crawl down them by grasping the tufts of grass growing from the coral. But these soldiers in the main force were carrying fifty pounds of personal equipment, plus the machine guns, grenade launchers, and the ammunition. There were no mules and all the division's horses had been left behind at Rabaul, so the heavy stuff—the 37mm anti-tank guns and the 70mm and 75mm fieldpieces—had to be manhandled. The only way to negotiate these cliffs was to lower the fieldpieces by rope. Such a slow process was impossible in the daylight with the American planes circling overhead like vultures, so most of the difficult work had to be done at night.

It soon became apparent that everyone must go on half rations, officers and men alike. Patriotism, love of country, kept them going. Often, when it seemed impossible to advance a step further without collapsing, the officers would lead their men in the singing of the "Kima Ga Yo," the national anthem. Facing in the direction of the homeland (or what they hoped was that direction), the men, tears streaming down their faces, would sing as loud as they could, and let the Yankee patrols be damned.

We know all these things because so much of it was recorded, again and again, in the diaries and the notebooks these men carried into battle with them, many of which we recovered and then translated into English.

By the twentieth, the forward units had finally crossed the Lunga, but so far upstream that six miles remained between them and the airfield. Still, the worst of the thirty-five-mile trek was over, and we were innocently unaware of their whereabouts.

Even at this late date, the Japanese were still bubbling with overconfidence. On the twenty-first, Maruyama instructed his units how to handle an American surrender. The Marines, he said, were to be told to lay down their arms and leave their supplies and equipment intact. Vandegrift, their commanding general, would be required to walk to the mouth of the Matanikau and surrender personally to General Hyakutake, who would be wearing his dress-white uniform.

Maruyama had planned that the main attack would be made by his Twenty-ninth Regiment, moving north over the same ridge that Kawaguchi had tried to storm in September. On the Twenty-ninth's left, the Sixteenth Regiment would drive toward Lunga Point along the west bank of the Lunga River, while over on the right, Kawaguchi, back once more at his old stamping ground, would push with about twenty-five hundred men to the eastern end of the airfield. Then, if all went well, a thousand men from Kokumbona would sneak along the coast in barges and make a direct landing at Lunga Point, landings being a Japanese specialty.

Thanks to all those overly optimistic reports, Maruyama had expected that his units would be ready to attack by late afternoon on the twenty-third. From high in the mountains the airfield looked tantalizingly close at hand, but down in the jungle ravines the men were barely moving. Now, too, heavy rains churned the ground into a quagmire, and the trails were so slippery that the slightest grade called for ropes. The result was the force was still bogged down on the twenty-third, and Maruyama had to postpone H-hour until 5 p.m. on the twenty-fourth.

It's understandable that the Twenty-ninth should have been chosen to lead the attack, for in the entire Japanese army no regiment's colors were more honored. An American observer, Lieutenant Colonel Warren Clear,

had once watched the unit make a practice march of 122 miles in sev-
enty-two hours and cross the finish line in double time.

But this time the Twenty-ninth was in trouble. When H-hour came,
the lead units were hopelessly lost, caught in the middle of a tremendous
rainstorm. An officer patrol was sent forward to find the enemy's location, but he could find nothing. It suddenly became clear to the unit's
commanding officer, Colonel Furimiya, that he and his troops were still
miles to the south of the airfield. It wasn't until midnight of the twenty-
fifth, thirty-one hours late, that Furimiya's forward units finally made
contact with the Americans.

Exhausted and confused, the Japanese became disoriented. Colonel
Shoji, with the right wing (it is still not clear if he was now in command,
in place of Kawaguchi, and he may not have known himself), veered off
to the northeast, and some of his troops more or less disappeared. But
one of his battalions, the First from the 230th Infantry, made contact
with Chesty Puller's First Battalion, Seventh Marines, close to midnight
on the twenty-fourth.

Puller realized he was facing a serious attack and called for reinforcements. By 2 a.m. on the twenty-fifth, National Guardsmen from the
164th Regiment had been led, sometimes by hand, into position with the
Marines.

The Japanese attack was led by a single company, the Eleventh, from
the Twenty-ninth Regiment's First Battalion, accompanied by, of all
things, the battalion's headquarters. Another company wandered off to
the left and made an attack of its own on American lines. The fighting
was blurred and confused, but the outcome was clear enough. Once
again, the Japanese were routed. In one small piece of the action, Marine
Sergeant John Basilone and his machine-gun section killed an entire
Japanese company in less than five minutes. Basilone was awarded a
Medal of Honor (and was himself killed on Iwo Jima).

By now, too, American artillery, shifting from the battle at the sandspit, was cutting down hundreds of Japanese soldiers.

Of all the captured Japanese diaries and notebooks, none is more
poignant than the one taken from the body of Colonel Furimiya, commanding officer of the Twenty-ninth Regiment. Furimiya actually penetrated the American lines with a handful of troops, carrying with them the
regiment's sacred colors. When the sun came up, Furimiya found he was
isolated, surrounded by Americans. "Those who followed me in the charge
. . . are the eight persons . . . whose names are written on the back of this

page"—Captain Suzuki, Lieutenant Ono, Warrant Officer Kobayashi, Sergeant Ogawa, Corporals Sato and Wakisawa, Lance Corporal Takahara, and Superior Privates Kondo and Sakamoto.

Furimiya described his efforts to make contact with other Japanese units to continue the attack, all of them failures. "There was an enemy signal station in this area. I considered attacking it, but we did not because I thought I would escape from here with my subordinates in case the main force did not arrive. I am ashamed of my lack of training."

At one point, while they were hiding in the jungle growth, "a friendly plane carried out a low-flight reconnaissance in the face of enemy machine guns. As I thought the plane was sent out by special arrangement of the division commander to hunt for us, we immediately signaled but the plane did not discover our position."

Furimiya lamented the lack of Japanese artillery fire against enemy positions. "Penetration of the enemy line can be easily accomplished by ordinary flanking neutralization fire. There is no need to be afraid."

Firepower was on his mind. "We must not overlook firepower," he wrote. "When there is firepower the troops become full of spirit but when firepower ceases they become inactive. Spirit exists externally."

Lieutenant Ono and two soldiers were sent to find an escape route through American lines, but they never came back. Warrant Officer Kobayashi was sent out to find them, but he never came back either.

"At daybreak [on the twenty-ninth] we gave up hope of escaping and began to make last preparations," which included tearing the colors into little bits and scattering them through the dense jungle vegetation.

"I am going to return my borrowed life today with short interest," he wrote. In a final note to General Maruyama, he said, "I do not know what excuse to give. I apologize for what I have done."

He then asked Captain Suzuki if he was ready. He said he was. Suzuki killed his colonel first, firing a shot into his temple, and then killed himself. The rest of the men dispersed, and two or three of them actually managed to get back to their own lines days later.

Maruyama, who had vowed he "would exterminate the enemy around the airfield in one blow," called off the attack and ordered a retreat. He had lost about thirty-five hundred men; more died later in the jungles, from sickness and from their wounds. The Americans, Marines and soldiers, lost about three hundred men. The Marines were especially grateful to the National Guardsmen from the 164th Regiment, who had fought so well at their side. Colonel Cates told the unit's commander,

Colonel Moore, that the First Marines "were proud to serve with such a unit as yours."

Then, too, as Colonel Cates wrote in his memoirs, "McKelvy's battalion finally received the credit that is due," joining the First and Second Battalions that had already been singled out for division commendation for their performance on the Tenaru.

"The Commanding General commends the Third Battalion, First Marines, for noteworthy performance of duty during the period 9 October 1942 to 1 November 1942," the citation read.

So McKelvy won what he had been looking for all along—recognition. And, truth to tell, the son of a bitch deserved it.

9

Winding Down

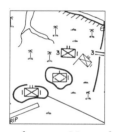

Our situation, so critical earlier, started to look up in November. For one thing, reinforcements began arriving in a steady stream. The Second Marines moved over to Guadalcanal from Tulagi on October 29 and 30, and the Eighth Marines arrived on November 4 and 5. Big guns—powerful 155mm weapons that could answer the Japanese 150mm Pistol Petes—came ashore on November 2.

We didn't know it, but the man responsible for our improved situation was FDR himself. Roosevelt told his service chiefs on October 24 that he wanted Guadalcanal moved to the top of the priority list, and it was. He also authorized *Time* magazine to put Vandegrift on its cover in early November. The general said he was pleased that the cover story "seemed to bring the real meaning of the campaign home to the American public." FDR remains a great hero to many of us.

But if we were doing better on the ground, the Navy was still having a tough time with the Japanese at sea. We lost the carrier *Hornet* at the Battle of Santa Cruz on October 26. Then, on the night of November 12–13, we lost two cruisers and four destroyers in a wild and confused fight at close quarters. We also lost both of our admirals, Callaghan and

Scott, and seven hundred men. The next night, in the one major battleship engagement of the war, the *South Dakota* was badly damaged but the Japanese battleship, *Kirishima,* was sunk.

But our greatest success was achieved by airplanes based at Henderson Field. They located ten Japanese transports near the Russell Islands, loaded with troops to reinforce Guadalcanal, and sank or wrecked them all. Only one ship managed to put soldiers ashore.

Historian Richard Frank concluded that the naval and air battle that raged around Guadalcanal in November "was a decisive American victory," but we paid a heavy price for it. "By sunrise of November 15," Frank wrote, "it was clear which path the war was destined to follow." Clear in retrospect, no doubt; not yet so clear to those of us, weary and sick, our uniforms in rags, still holding our positions on Guadalcanal.

We weren't getting any help, either, from that strange and curious admiral, Kelly Turner, who was still giving Vandegrift and our top commanders on Guadalcanal fits. This time he came up with a simply terrible idea; he wanted to build an airfield in swamps near Aola Bay, fifty miles east of Lunga Point. Troops and Seabee construction workers needed elsewhere were diverted to Aola. In two weeks, it became obvious—just as Turner had been told—that there was no way to build an airfield in that kind of swampy terrain. The idea was abandoned.

Vandegrift, backed now by reinforcements that he said "gave me riches beyond the dreams of avarice," wanted to move west of the Matanikau River in the direction of Kokumbona. "By pushing to this line," he said, "I would force Hyakutake to use landing beaches much farther west besides freeing Henderson Field from Pistol Pete's harassing fire."

He assigned Edson's Fifth Marines, Colonel John M. Arthur's Second Marines (minus one battalion), the Third Battalion of the Seventh Marines, plus Whaling's sniper-scouts, supported by artillery, air, and surface units, to the task. "Such an attack force was certainly new to the Guadalcanal veterans," he wrote. "I could scarcely believe myself that we could muster it."

They moved rapidly toward Point Cruz, eventually enveloping the Japanese position. Major Lewis Walt (he would one day be a general in Vietnam) and his Second Battalion, Fifth Marines, caught 350 Japanese soldiers in a pocket and killed them all, capturing three cannons, nine 37mm guns, and thirty-two heavy and light machine guns. At about the same time, Captain Erskine Wells led his company in what the historians say remains the only authenticated bayonet charge of the campaign.

The "New Breed"—the author, in prewar riding boots, in a formal portrait taken a few days after his graduation from Marine Corps Officers Candidate School, at Quantico, Virginia.
(*Author's collection*)

The "Old Breed"—Lieutenant Colonel William N. "Wild Bill" McKelvy, commanding officer of the author's Third Battalion, a veteran of the Marines' "banana wars." *(Marine Corps Historical Center)*

The author's intelligence section, in a group photograph taken in the final days of the campaign. The author, in a toothbrush moustache, is front-row center. *(Author's collection)*

The Marines' often-underrated commander, Major General Archer Vandegrift (*far left*), confers with his staff onboard the USS *McCawley* (the author's transport too) as the Marines near their target.
(*National Archives*)

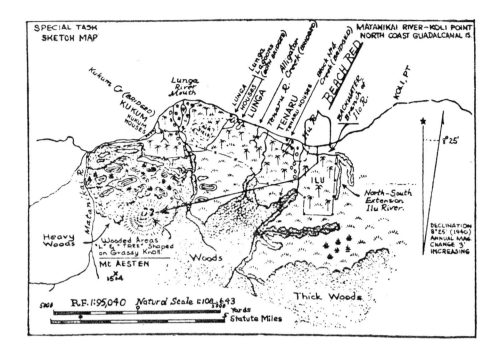

Cartographic & Reproduction Unit, Combat Team No.5 1242

Prepared under the direction of the Commander Combat Team No.5;1942.From Special Sketch
submitted,and controlled by Map;North Coast of Guadalcanal Island,R.F.1:95,040;14 July,1942

SPECIAL NOTE: This map was reproduced from Special Sketch Map drawn from the information
supplied by a man thoroughly familiar with the terrain shown. It is an approximate pic-
torial representation drawn from this person's memory.It is not to be construed as being
an accurate map.

: SYMBOLS :

`ᵒᵔᵔᵒ` DEEP DITCHES,WITH HOLES   `ı'''ı ı'''ı` GRASS PLAINS (THICK:4TO 6 FT.HIGH)

`ᴬ ᴬ` SWAMP   `⌒` KNOLLS   `·ıı T ıı·` COCONUT PALMS AND GRASS LAND

`x—x—` FIVE STRAND BARBED WIRE FENCES   `—o—o` FENCE. (TEN YEAR OLD)
    (GOOD REPAIR)

BRIDGES. 3 TON LIMIT. ONE WAY TRAFFIC

KUKUM,LUNGA,TENARU and ILU,are Plantations

This crudely drawn and wildly inaccurate map, based on information supplied by
a civilian who said he was familiar with the island's north coast, was all the
Marines in the field had to work with when they made their landing.
(Marine Corps Historical Center)

McKelvy, the grand strategist, studying maps he could barely read in his rude jungle command post.
(National Archives)

The Marines had at least one friend on Guadalcanal—Sergeant Major Jacob Vouza, formerly of the Solomons constabulary. The author greeted him when, badly wounded, he staggered into the Marines' lines. (*National Archives*)

The Marines' deadliest weapon on Guadalcanal was field artillery. The Japanese had no inkling of the devastation these guns would cause when they laid down concentrated fire.
(National Archives)

The grisliest of all Guadalcanal photographs—Ichiki's Japanese dead, buried in the sand, after the Battle of the Tenaru, August 21. Marine artillery inflicted most of the damage.
(*National Archives*)

The Japanese attack on McKelvy's position at the sandspit at the mouth of the Matanikau on October 22 was led by these light and medium tanks, the only time the Japanese used tanks in the whole campaign. They were all destroyed, and McKelvy finally won the recognition he had craved.
(National Archives)

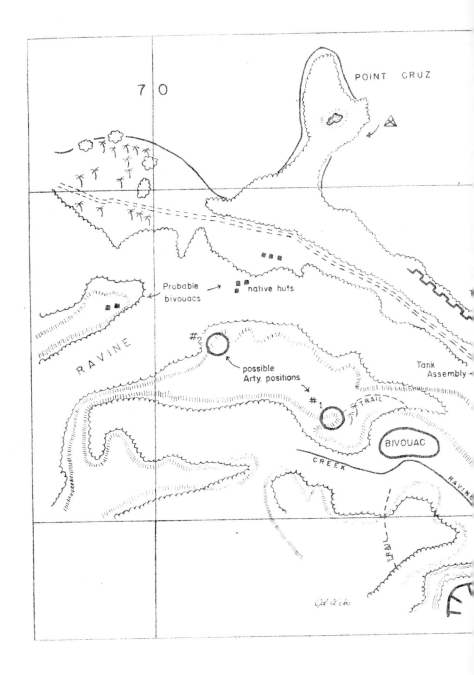

POINT CRUZ

7 0

Probable → ■ ■ native huts
bivouacs

RAVINE

#2 possible
Arty. positions
#1

Tank
Assembly

TRAIL

BIVOUAC

CREEK

RAVINE

TRAIL

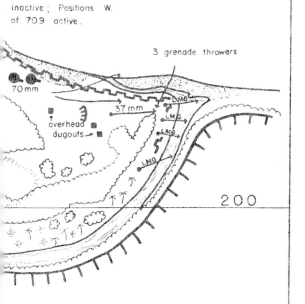

SITUATION SKETCH
10/28/42
T. SEC. 3d BN FIRST MARINES

201

Positions E. of 70.9
inactive ; Positions W.
of 70.9 active.

3 grenade throwers

70 mm

37 mm

LMG

LMG

LMG

overhead
dugouts

LMG

200

A map drawn after Ramrod Taylor's death shows the situation as he knew it when he and his patrol set out to destroy the Japanese guns labeled "#1 and #2, possible Arty. positions," near map's center.
(*Marine Corps Gazette*)

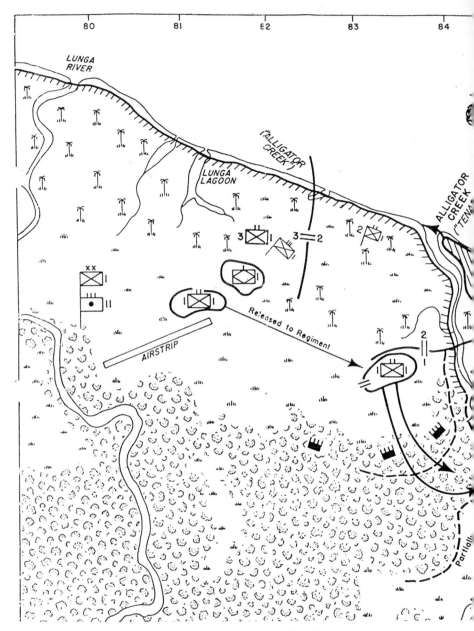

Official Marine Corps map, drawn after the battle, shows position of Ichiki's Detachment before it was wiped out at the Battle of the Tenaru, August 21. (*Marine Corps Historical Center*)

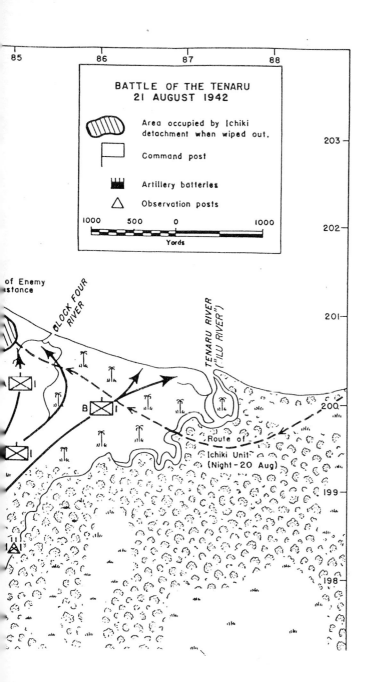

85   86   87   88

BATTLE OF THE TENARU
21 AUGUST 1942

Area occupied by Ichiki
detachment when wiped out.

Command post

Artillery batteries

Observation posts

1000   500   0   1000

Yards

203 —

202 —

201 —

200 —

199 —

198 —

of Enemy
istance

BLOCK FOUR RIVER

TENARU RIVER
("ILU RIVER")

B

Route of
Ichiki Unit
(Night - 20 Aug)

A

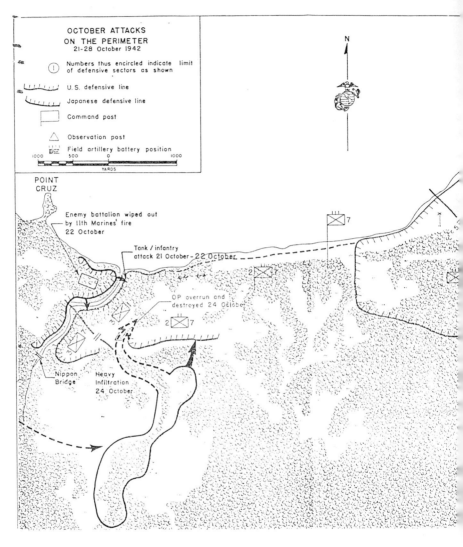

N

POINT
CRUZ

Enemy battalion wiped out
by 11th Marines' fire
22 October

Tank / infantry
attack 21 October - 22 October

OP overrun and
destroyed 24 October

Nippon   Heavy
Bridge   Infiltration
24 October

This Marine Corps map, "October Attacks on the Perimeter," shows the position of the author's battalion at the time of the October 22 tank attack at the Matanikau sandspit (*far left*). It also gives a clear picture of the Marine position, including Henderson Field.
(*Marine Corps Historical Center*)

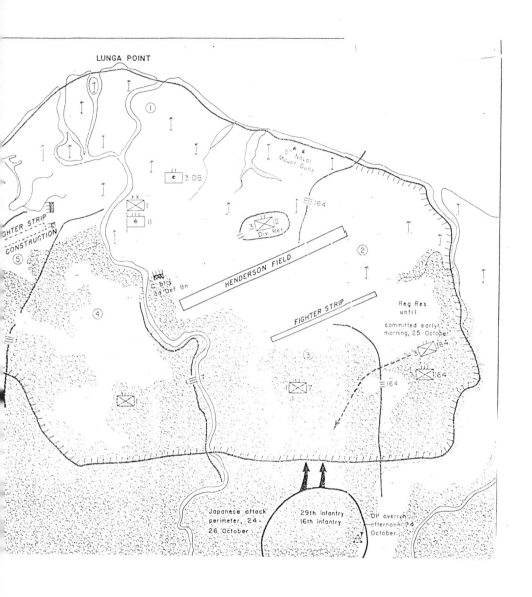

LUNGA POINT

Naval
Mount Guns

3 DB

164

3 11 2
Div Res

C BTG
3d Def Bn

HENDERSON FIELD

FIGHTER STRIP
CONSTRUCTION

FIGHTER STRIP

Reg Res
until
committed early
morning, 25 October

3 164

164

164

7

Japanese attack
perimeter, 24 -
26 October

29th infantry
16th infantry

OP overrun
afternoon, 24
October

Our role in all of this was to put out those patrols I described in Chapter 7 that led to the unfortunate, and we all felt, unnecessary, death of my friend, Ramrod Taylor.

As offensives go, this one was pretty much on track until we learned that the Japanese were gathering in strength on our eastern flank, just the opposite direction, near Koli Point. Vandegrift was forced to call off the attack across the Matanikau and rush troops to meet the new threat.

"Terrain, general fatigue of troops and combat inexperience of the Army units" hampered the plan to envelop the Japanese, and most of them managed to escape west, Vandegrift reported.

There were about three thousand of these soldiers, under the command of Colonel Shoji, and their aim was to move through the jungle to the east, where they hoped to join up with what was left of the once mighty Seventeenth Army.

It was at this point that the most eccentric of all the Marines' officers (and that's saying quite a lot), Lieutenant Colonel Evans F. Carlson, made his bid for glory on Guadalcanal. He had recently arrived on the island with his Second Raider Battalion, and he brought with him his own notions of warfare. He had served with the Communist Chinese Eighth Route Army, learning all about guerrilla warfare and adopting the Chinese slogan "Gung ho!," meaning "Work together!"

Most of us didn't entirely approve of Carlson's outfit or his methods of going to war. But we probably shared the sentiment once expressed by David Shoup, a future Marine commandant, and related in Frank's history of Guadalcanal: "He may have been Red but he wasn't yellow."

All of his men had volunteered to be Raiders, and each of them had answered Carlson's question in the affirmative: "Do you think you could cut a Jap's throat without flinching?"

What happened now was that Carlson took his Raiders in pursuit of Shoji's desperate troops in a kind of private war that lasted for thirty days. In that time, the official Marine report stated, these Raiders fought no less than twelve successful actions and had counted enemy dead in excess of four hundred. Their losses, sixteen dead, were surprisingly small.

Shoji made it back to the Seventeenth Army with less than eight hundred men, of whom only a handful remained fit for duty. Dramatic stuff, we agreed, but for all of that a sideshow.

We were still manning our lines, and during the last two weeks of November we had almost no contact with the enemy. "December and we're still here," I wrote Dad and Margaret on December 2. "I never thought I'd be sleeping under a tree in the Christmas season! It's actually better now than it was several months ago. However, the nights are very cool—so cool in fact that I sleep under a blanket. We have two marvelous places to swim here. One river comes right down out of the mountains to the south and is very clear. We wash our clothes there so they are dry by the time we're through swimming."

I said in that letter the Navy "has been doing a swell job here. We've been able to see all of the naval battles even if it's only flashes from the guns and the dull rumble of explosions. Every once in a while a ship blows up and that's a pretty sight."

That, in hindsight, was a generous estimate of the Navy's performance, for the troubles at sea still hadn't ended. On November 30, a powerful American task force led by Rear Admiral Carleton Wright met a small force of Japanese destroyers led by Rear Admiral Raizo Tanaka, and the Americans were badly defeated in a battle—called Tassafaronga—that historian Frank called "a humiliation." Put plainly, he said, "an inferior, cargo-entangled, and partly surprised destroyer squadron had demolished a superior cruiser-destroyer group." Navy historian Samuel Eliot Morison said our marksmanship that night was "abominable." Still, thanks to Wright's intervention, none of the supplies Admiral Tanaka was hoping to land on Guadalcanal got ashore, and that was a tremendous blow to the enemy.

From captured diaries we had some idea of just how badly things were going for the Japanese infantrymen still clinging to their positions on Guadalcanal. We found this one on the body of a truck driver, probably attached to the Forty-third Infantry Division:

> Because of hunger and weariness, I can't go on. Ah! There is machine-gun fire from morning til night! I can't express my feelings. I can't smoke even one cigaret or eat one grain of rice. Everyone is worn out. When shall we be rescued? The people at home cannot understand this suffering. . . .
>
> Ah! From today we go to dig potatoes and to gather coconuts, with which to sustain our lives. Sometimes, there are sweet potatoes in the mountains and we eat them, vines and all. Really, I never imagined I would experience such a life.
>
> All the soldiers, wherever they are walking, go staggering along. This is hell's front line!

Our time on Guadalcanal was running down. As early as November 16, Vandegrift was told by Admiral Turner that the evacuation of the First Marine Division might get under way as early as November 26. Vandegrift wasn't opposed to that, but in a letter to a Marine colleague he said he would like to know just where his Marines were to be sent. Should we return to Wellington, in New Zealand, he said, "we have a setup already there. If it is to be Auckland or some other new place, certain staff officers should precede the first contingent and make necessary arrangements."

Vandegrift agreed it was a good idea to leave his division's heavy equipment behind for the Army reinforcements, including the amphibious tractors. They "are shot," he said, though "they have paid for themselves one hundred times over."

The key decision was reached on November 29, when the Army's Twenty-fifth Division was ordered to proceed to Guadalcanal (instead of Australia, where it had been headed).

On December 7, the first anniversary of the terrible disaster at Pearl Harbor, Vandegrift issued his final letter to his men on Guadalcanal:

> I hope that in some small measure I can convey to you my feeling of pride in your magnificent accomplishments and my thanks for the unbounded loyalty, limitless self-sacrifice and high courage which have made those accomplishments possible. To the soldiers and Marines who have faced the enemy in the fierceness of night and combat . . . whose unbelievable accomplishments have made the name "Guadalcanal" a synonym for death and disaster in the language of our enemy . . . I say that at all times you have faced without flinching the worst that the enemy could do to us and have thrown back the best that he could send against us.

Two days later, Vandegrift handed over command of American troops on Guadalcanal to Army Major General Alexander M. Patch, commanding general of the Americal Division, the only division in the U.S. Army without a number (it was formed, mostly of National Guardsmen, in New Caledonia). The Marines on the island were now represented by the newly arrived Second Marine Division (though one of its regiments, the Second, had been there all along). Vandegrift headed home, where he was decorated with the Medal of Honor by President Roosevelt and where he soon became the new commandant of the Marine Corps.

McKelvy and the rest of us in the Third Battalion left Guadalcanal on December 15, with the other units in the regiment departing a week later.

Most of us took some time before we left to visit the Marine graveyard. We held a final memorial service on the fourteenth. After the ceremony was over, we fanned out to tidy up the 650 grave sites.

We were exhausted and sick and we looked like hell. Our regimental commander, Colonel Cates, described our appearance this way:

> I wish that I could paint a vivid word picture of the men as they loaded into the boats. The phrase, "The raggedy-assed Marines are on parade," comes as near describing them as possible. Hats and caps of every description, tattered and torn shirts (some bareback), trousers of every kind (some cut off so short that they looked like "G" strings), badly worn shoes of all kinds (a few Japanese sneakers), and very few had underwear and socks. Surprisingly enough, almost everyone had his weapon and gas mask, and, most remarkable of all, they were all in very good condition. A good Marine—and they are excellent Marines—always takes good care of his arms, even if everything else goes to pot.

The fighting went on for weeks after we left Guadalcanal, and some Army veterans of the campaign still complain that they've been short-changed for what they accomplished after we had gone. The fighting didn't end until February 9.

Military historians may argue (and some do) that the fighting on Guadalcanal was simply a series of small-unit actions that can't really be compared to many of the great battles of World War II. The final count showed that we lost 1,207 Marines and 562 soldiers in ground action on Guadalcanal, out of more than 50,000 who took part. The Navy lost even more men at sea, almost 5,000. Historian Frank estimated that the total of killed and permanently missing on land, sea, and air for the United States was 7,100. Japanese casualties were much heavier—25,600 soldiers on the ground, 3,543 men at sea, and 1,200 in the air (including some of the best pilots Japan had).

But when the war was over, both sides, American and Japanese, agreed that Guadalcanal was the true turning point in the war in the Pacific. This is where we discovered we could meet these tough Japanese troops in the most adverse conditions—and beat them. "Guadalcanal," Admiral Morison wrote, "is not a name but an emotion, recalling desperate fights in the air, furious night naval battles, savage fighting in the sodden jungle nights broken by screaming bombs and deafening explosions of naval shells."

Historian Frank concluded his definitive account of the campaign by quoting these words from James Michener:

> They will live a long time, these men of the South Pacific. They had an American quality. They, like their victories, will be remembered as long as our generation lives. After that, like the men of the Confederacy, they will become strangers. Longer and longer shadows will obscure them, until their Guadalcanal sounds distant on the ear like Shiloh and Valley Forge.

So we were heroes, and in time we would become legends. But what we remembered most was that we had done our job, and that we were heading back to civilization—to clean sheets, new uniforms, big steaks, beer, and women.

And, from now on, we could wear what I told Dad and Margaret was a very nice shoulder insignia—"a blue diamond with white stars on it (the Southern Cross) and on it a red '1' with Guadalcanal printed down it. Quite snappy, and do the Marines stick out their chests when the 'dogfaces' [GIs] pass by!"

10

Recuperating

Brisbane, where we had been sent to recuperate, was bad duty. We were encamped in a former Australian army barracks, the only notable feature being a band of ferocious ants.

One of the problems—at least as we saw it—was that we were now under the command of the Army general we considered to be our nemesis—Douglas MacArthur. We called him, uncharitably, "Dugout Doug."

MacArthur wanted us to stay in that awful camp near Brisbane, miles from town with only limited public transportation. Vandegrift complained to MacArthur, and then he complained again—seriously—when he learned on December 21 from his own surgeons that the camp was smack in the middle of an anopheline mosquito area, the kind that carry malaria, despite Army assurances to the contrary. In his letter to MacArthur, Vandegrift pointed out the malaria problem, and MacArthur finally consented to a move to a healthier camp farther south. But he added this in his letter to Vandegrift: "No transportation facilities are available in the Southwest Pacific area to effect the move which will have to be carried out by shipping made available from the South Pacific area." It's no wonder Marine veterans still nurse a grudge about that man.

Unable to get help from MacArthur, Vandegrift turned to Admiral Halsey, who agreed immediately to provide shipping for us from Brisbane to Melbourne, and to disembark all troops still returning from Guadalcanal at Melbourne. Not just any shipping either: Halsey gave us the *West Point,* formerly the great passenger liner *America,* to take us from Brisbane to Melbourne.

We'd had an awful time at Brisbane, a town filled with deskbound Air Corps, Navy, and Army officers. My men, having determined that a group of American nurses was quartered in a camp the other side of a nearby river, had planned a Christmas reception, and the nurses had agreed to participate. On the day before Christmas, it rained. The nurses said, sorry we can't make it. So a glum bunch of Marines sat out the holiday, blaming us, the officers, for letting them down badly.

Melbourne was great duty, and no Guadalcanal veteran will ever forget the time we spent there. It's a fine old Victorian city, and for us an amazingly social one. With my friends Ronnie Slay and Gerry Gage, I rented an apartment at 56 Jolimont Terrace, by the Yarra River. Parties were given for us all the time, thanks to a fine alliance between the Marines and Melbourne's leading social arbiter, Lady Clapp. George Hunt and I—we would one day work for Henry Luce at Time Inc.—shared many of these pressing social responsibilities.

Melbourne seemed to take us to its municipal heart—a local paper called us "The Saviors of Australia"—because it hadn't seen many servicemen or much wartime activity at that time. We did everything we could to change all that—even affecting swagger sticks, in the British imperial tradition.

In a letter to Dad and Margaret, I noted we had just had "our regimental dance the other evening at the Officers' Cabaret," formerly the city's leading nightclub. "All the gals came in evening gowns and it was quite an affair. We had a floor show from talent from enlisted men in the regiment. And they were surprisingly good. It was really done in style—engraved invitations, good service, excellent orchestra, good decorations—and even a receiving line! (regimental commander and Exec.) My, what a faraway place Guadalcanal seems like now!

"Our regiment has the reputation of being the 'social' outfit of the division. For one thing we're here in town and, in addition to the use of the elegant Division Club (canopy over the entrance and everything), we have our regimental Officers' Club which is a nice place to entertain. There are all sorts of official parties, promotions, etc., and the upper crust frequently throws parties for us. We're really leading the 'life of Riley' now, even though we're training fairly intensively. One of these days, though, we'll be going back to cold canned rations, and mosquitoes again, so we can enjoy ourselves now without having a guilty conscience."

For me, and for many others, the problem stemmed from those damned mosquitoes. I was still subject to recurring bouts with malaria, and would be for several years more. The doctors came to respect me as something of a medical star. I seemed to have chronic infections that were quite resistant to the standard treatment. The good part was sick leave. At one point I was sent, along with two other Marine officers, by night ferry to a hospital in what had been a Miami-like tourist hotel, called the Wrest Point Inn, on the island of Tasmania off the southern coast of Australia.

"Got out of the hospital last week," I wrote, "after a marvelous two-week sick leave. . . . Everyone was most hospitable. We were asked out everywhere—golf, tennis, yachting, and to the different clubs there. The girls were very pretty—beautiful complexions, but a bit too much like the old country to suit me. I haven't seen one yet that can dress half as well as a hometown shop girl. They just ain't got no style."

In Melbourne, I dated a girl who had come out, as a debutante, "several years ago at the Court of St. James's in London and hasn't recovered since. They certainly fawn over titles here." Thus spake an unreconstructed, small-d democratic rebel from Pennsylvania's Brandywine Valley.

After we had been there a few weeks, almost every Marine had managed to become involved in some kind of love affair with an Australian girl. We joked about our good fortune, of course; what soldier hasn't? I still have in my files a phoney "Application for a Date with a Marine," compiled by some of our Marines. "Figure," one section is headlined. "Good? Fair? Poor?" Another: "If you live at home, indicate on diagram exact position of parents' bedroom, light switch, davenport, back door, nearest open window." Still one more: "What do you estimate your capacity for the following to be? Wine? Scotch? Beer? Bourbon? Gin? (Nix on that 'champagne stuff.' You are not Grable and I'm not drawing general's pay yet)."

In the midst of the Marines' happy stay in Melbourne, the Aussies' crack Ninth Infantry Division returned home from the Middle East on a well-deserved furlough. "It's an excellent outfit with a fine record," I told

Dad and Margaret, "but the inevitable clash came due to our men's propensity for proclaiming to all that one member of our division can take on ten of any other." I also said I figured they were "a little peeved at having all their girls stolen from them."

We finally put an end to all the arguments and pub brawls by throwing a huge beer party for the "Desert Rats" at the city's biggest sports stadium. There were forty-five hundred of us and an equal number of them. To be on the safe side, the beer was served in paper cups instead of bottles. The party was a huge success.

There was serious business, some of the time. I got the job I wanted most—R-2, regimental intelligence officer, and was assigned with George Hunt to run the division's scout and sniper school up in the Dandenong hills. It was a good school, but I must say that teaching Marines how to read maps is a difficult chore. We had a special problem—Navajo Indians. They had been signed up, and were now taking our course, because somebody with a much higher rank figured that their language would be so unintelligible to the enemy (to us, too) that they could send rapid-fire messages to each other in their native language without any need for encoding and decoding.

But these Indians were a very unhappy lot, homesick for their reservations, and we were still looking for a way to make them feel accepted by the Marines. It didn't work with us, but eventually somebody figured it out, for these Marine Indians performed notable work at Iwo Jima and other fierce battlegrounds.

I was unhappy too, because I simply couldn't shake that malaria bug. So, in the end, with other Marines in the same condition, I was ordered home to the United States. We sailed on an old Italian ship called the *Conte Biancomo,* known to us as Mussolini's Revenge. It had a most disconcerting way of stopping dead in the water, and for much longer than it took to fix the machinery. On such occasions, jokers in our midst bawled out orders, in what they felt was a Japanese accent, to fire when ready.

I was a very busy person, being the senior of just a handful of Marine officers on board the ship. But I was in luck. The senior noncommissioned officer was none other than Master Gunnery Sergeant Lou Diamond (he had malaria too), and the two of us took turns as officer of the deck.

Diamond personified the Marines' "Old Breed." He was a legend, and the men whispered he was a hundred years old. No such thing; no one ever knew his exact age, but he probably was somewhere between sixty and sixty-five when I first met him. He was, first and foremost, a mortar man, and his weapon of choice was the 81mm weapon. It was said he could drop a mortar round down the funnel of an enemy warship. In maneuvers back home, it was said, he actually had dropped a round down a chimney. There may not be a word of truth to any of these stories, but they were important all the same. Marines very much wanted to believe anything that reinforced their faith in their own military prowess.

Diamond was not much to look at. He wasn't tall and, from his prodigious intake of beer, had a prominent belly. His uniforms were a little rumpled, and, because he was Lou Diamond, he wore a long beard (in itself a break with tradition; normally, he fancied a small goatee).

Lou's toughest assignment was maintaining strict discipline on the boat ride home, no easy task given the fact we were carrying—for reasons I can't recall—a great many young Polish girls, whom the Marines considered fair game. Also on board were seven hundred missionaries, from God knows where, and they were simply obnoxious. To our dismay, they felt they should have the best of everything, and they took it.

Lou really ran the ship, and he did it with great élan. "Begging your pardon," he would say to me from time to time, "but shouldn't we have the men fall in now?" Sure we should, and when he said so, the men fell in.

Missionaries, Polish girls, and Marines, we finally got . . . home.

11

Teaching

And so here I was, in July of 1943, back home in West Chester, on sick leave, with nothing to do.

I figured, if I couldn't fight, maybe I could teach. I fired off a letter to my old regimental commander on Guadalcanal, Colonel Cates, now a brigadier general commanding the Marine Corps Schools at Quantico, where I had joined the Marines in what seemed a different lifetime.

"As you may recall," I wrote, "I served under your command as Bn-2 of the Third Battalion throughout the campaign. In Australia I held a map reading course for the Regimental Intelligence sections and the Snipers . . . and later was instructor in mapping, terrain, etc., at Lt. Col. Buckley's Division Scout School at Balcombe."

Now comes the pitch: "On the basis of the above experience I should very much like to be considered for a post at the Marine Corps Schools as an instructor in Intelligence. . . . I have brought back all of the photos, mosaics, maps and sketches we had of Guadalcanal [and] the complete intelligence files of the 3d Bn. . . . as illustrative material."

I heard from Cates a week later. The pitch worked. "It will be a pleasure," he said, "to have you here in the Schools. We have quite a few of the old outfit, and I must admit we are finding the duty here very desirable."

I arrived at Quantico in September—a teacher, and my subject would be the Guadalcanal campaign, with special attention to our enemy, the Japanese, as a fighting man. But first I had to take a three-month course on how to teach like a West Point professor. "The school started today," I wrote Dad and Margaret. "There are about 60 of us—mostly Lt. Colonels and Majors. There are about 20 captains. As I am about the most junior Captain here I am almost the lowest ranking officer in the school. Fortunately there is one lower than I—he has to take the roll call, etc., and other additional duties. Classes start at 8:00 and end at 4:30 (including Saturdays). The course sounds fascinating and is quite tough."

I said at the time it was as demanding as anything I had known in the Ivy League, and it was.

A good thing, too, for, when it came time to lecture, I was faced with some very bright students—a major in the British Marines, an English major from the Berkshire regiment, an Australian lieutenant colonel, a New Zealand captain, a Dutch lieutenant commander, and two Dutch Marine majors. I also noted in a letter to my old headmaster and his wife, Walden and Edith Pell, that the class contained some "furriners" too—officers from our own Army and Navy.

My message to these professionals was pretty basic—the Japanese could have won the battle for Guadalcanal. The reason they failed stemmed from their own shortcomings. These shortcomings were endemic, and they persisted long after Guadalcanal.

Most striking, I said, was the way the Japanese underestimated us. This didn't make a whole lot of sense. Americans aren't all that peaceable. We virtually invented modern warfare in our own Civil War, fighting each other. Our commanding general's grandfather, Carson Vandegrift, fought on the Confederate side with the Monticello Guards and was wounded twice, at Antietam and in Pickett's charge at Gettysburg. More Americans died in a few hours in some of these terrible battles than fell in the whole Guadalcanal campaign.

We captured a Japanese document in which some of their planners attempted to assess our capabilities. "National unity is fairly strong," the writers conceded. "They like novelty and are adventurous." But "although they are optimistic, they lack perseverance." Most damaging, they said: "The American soldier, without support of firepower, is easily overcome and in combat is easily made to throw up his hands and sur-render. If wounded, he immediately raises a cry of distress, etc. He lacks hand-to-hand fighting ability and spiritual strength. However, with the support of firepower, he gets fairly aggressive."

The business about surrendering is curious. The fact is, Marines didn't surrender—ever—on Guadalcanal. On the other hand, we managed to capture a number of Japanese soldiers, all of them carrying revealing diaries and almost all of them willing to answer just about any question we asked them.

"To sum up," these Japanese analysts said, "the enemy's military preparations may be said to be built on a framework of a materialistically organized firepower with the benefits of air activity added. They are never seen to maintain any particular fighting power, and although they are at present exerting themselves in the extreme and strengthening their posi-tions, if we make especially thorough preparations, prepare our fighting strength to deal hammerlike blows against the enemy, concentrating on using all sorts of original plans and carry them out with a flourishing aggressive spirit, our success in the present operation is certainly beyond doubt."

The spiritual and moral dimension was critical, for the Japanese fig-ured they had the upper hand on this score. Americans, they believed, were materialistic—they know all about automobiles and engines, one analysis noted, but they would never be able to survive banzai attacks with Japanese officers and soldiers wielding swords and bayonets because they didn't have the fortitude to stand up against men with such spiri-tual dedication, men so willing to die for their emperor and the glorious traditions of their fighting units. It was mostly nonsense, yet many high-ranking Japanese officers believed it.

But of course not all Japanese officers were fools. We captured a young one, Second Lieutenant Togo Tokunaga, near Mt. Austen. He had been wounded twice and was too weak and sick to go on. At the time of his capture, the report by his interviewers said, he tried "to end his life with a hand grenade which failed to explode."

Unlike most captured officers, he was talkative during his interviews. He said that for many days leading to his capture he and his men had only a little rice and bean paste to eat, but no canned goods. He said this was because the men were too tired to go down to the beach for supplies. He said that when he was taken to the field hospital, he learned there were virtually no medical supplies, except some iodine.

As for the men who led him and his unit—he was a part of the ubiquitous Colonel Oka's outfit—he had nothing but contempt. Their overwhelming defeat at the Matanikau River, he said, was due to sheer stupidity on the part of the Japanese commanders who never gave the Americans credit for having artillery sufficient to withstand a tank attack, and never employed any of the principles of battle tactics which were taught to every junior officer starting with his indoctrination into the service.

We couldn't have agreed more. In the Division Commander's *Final Report on the Guadalcanal Operation, Phase IV,* our analysts concluded that in these early operations covered by the report, "the enemy grossly underestimated either our strength, our fighting qualities, or both. It may be that his earlier successes against white troops in eastern theaters had induced a state of contempt for our capacity or willingness to fight. In any event he was thoroughly beaten at every point of contact and in the final analysis showed that he was utterly incapable, intellectually and morally, of meeting the requirements of modern warfare."

This, of course, isn't what most of us had been led to expect. The Japanese armies had been triumphant, and the free world recognized Japanese soldiers and armies as tough, resourceful, patriotic, and immensely skilled at the kind of jungle warfare we faced on Guadalcanal. We presumed that their commanding officers, most of them combat veterans, knew precisely what they were doing.

General Hyakutake, the commander of the Seventeenth Army, seemed to understand what was required. In a proclamation issued to his men on August 28, just three weeks after we landed, he said the operation to recapture Guadalcanal "is a truly important one which will determine supremacy in the whole Pacific area. Already," he said, "the main force of the Ichiki Detachment and the Naval Guard units are at Guadalcanal and stoutly maintaining their positions."

He recognized shortcomings in preparing for the battle. "Although I know that your units' organization, transportation essentials, etc., are not always satisfactory, the war situation does not permit a moment's delay." So, he concluded, "relying upon the skill of command and the power of combination, strike with our strong points against their weak points. Inflict severe blows upon the enemy, whose infantry probably is not toughened to that land as yet, and expect to annihilate them. Battles always pass through grave turning points. The glory of victory will be returned to one who looks up to it and always believes in it."

What he was saying was perfectly sensible. He understood that Guadalcanal was going to be a turning point, even though some Japanese strategists didn't. And, yes, many of his troops would be veterans and so it would be wise for them to strike before the Marines had become accustomed to the jungle and to the battlefield. And, of course, strike with overwhelming power at the enemy's weakest points.

Hyakutake mentioned the Ichiki Detachment in his proclamation. These were fine, hardened Japanese troops, but more than seven hundred of Ichiki's nine hundred men died in the Battle of the Tenaru in an attack so willfully stupid that it still boggles the mind. Ichiki had actually taught infantry tactics and commanded troops in China, but here were nine hundred men attacking as many as ten thousand Marines, surely not a matter of striking the enemy's weakest points with your strongest force. As Cates said over and over again, it was just plain stupid.

Massed American firepower, plus attacks by American aircraft, something the Japanese never anticipated, made the difference. It would do so, again and again, throughout the campaign, and Japanese diaries and prisoner interviews tell of the horror of those barrages almost endlessly.

I used First Lieutenant Hisatomi's diary in my lectures because it is so complete and so informative. He was an extraordinarily intelligent and sensitive Japanese soldier, and his diary tells us more about what was happening to the enemy, and in the enemy's mind, than almost any other document I have seen. Hisatomi was commanding officer of the Second Company in the First Battalion of the 124th Infantry Regiment and took part in the actions that culminated in the furious battle for Edson's Ridge the night of September 13 and 14 that I described in chapter 6.

At dawn on September 2, the day Hisatomi and his unit took up positions on Guadalcanal, they were attacked by American aircraft. "Although all the troops deployed themselves in the jungle, there were casualties among them. I myself received near misses from these bombings and strafings. The enemy continued his bombing attacks almost all day long—four times in the morning and twice in the afternoon. Therefore, I stayed in the trench all day. I haven't any appetite. Although I think that these bombings are a test of intestinal fortitude, it is maddening to be the recipient of these daring and insulting attacks by the American forces."

On September 6, Hisatomi said, "Our life in the trenches is overwhelmed with rain. The men who are cooking and those performing miscellaneous duties are constantly wet. I worry these men will take cold. It rained almost all night. Occasionally the enemy planes fly overhead. Life is now drab. We are waiting only the order for the general attack."

September 8: "It has been raining since morning. The sky is overcast. At about 0700, we hear through the rain the roar of the guns from enemy ships resounding from the point of our landing. It seems that the enemy has planned a landing. The report . . . states that 2,000 enemy troops landed near the point [Kokumbona] where we disembarked and captured our AA guns."

Hungry and weary, Hisatomi and his men began their advance that afternoon and reached the point where they hoped to launch a night attack against American positions on September 12. "The battalion commander [Major Yukichi Kokusho] assembled all the company commanders and gave us our orders. As soon as dusk fell we began our march along the river. . . . When we had advanced about two kilometers, we encountered the enemy's front line and received heavy hostile gun fire. . . . We have no knowledge of the terrain nor the enemy position." The first attack was driven back, and Hisatomi's company, along with all the others, was forced to withdraw.

At 1300 the next day, the thirteenth, "all company commanders were assembled by the battalion commander. He said that he had given deep consideration to the present situation. He gave us a spirited talk stating that this was a difficult operation and we must sacrifice our lives to serve our Emperor and our country. He issued orders for the second attack."

What happened next is very revealing. "At 1400, the advance party departed. Annihilating the opposing outposts on the way, they advanced toward the prearranged position. In the dark the enemy's front-line gun position, which was protected by barbed wire, was captured." So far, everything is going as planned. But then this: "The battalion concentrated at this point, but received a terrific enemy artillery barrage. Casualties were heavy in all companies, and every unit scattered."

It was a disaster. "We suffered enormous casualties due to the accurate artillery barrage and strafing of the enemy. The battalion commander, five other officers and approximately 180 men were killed. More than 100 men were injured so badly that they had to be carried on litters. There were countless numbers of men who were hit but still able to walk. The transporting of so many patients by only a small number of men who were physically sound created a very difficult problem. The rations had been completely exhausted by the end of the night attack. Although it was possible to march two or three days on the difficult road without food, the men were tiring from hunger, day by day. It was a very pitiful sight. We took three days to evacuate to a [safe] point. . . .

"We had never experienced this retreat march in the China Incident and it is a very distressing event. When I read this diary in the future I believe I'll be carried away with some deep emotions. The faithful heroes in battlefields are not always found in the attack, but also in the distressing aftermath. The sight of these men who are enduring hardships and hunger, the kind of affections of transporting the wounded, is even more beautiful than the picture of them in victory.

"These are the qualities of only the faithful and well-trained armies. I cannot help from crying when I see the sight of these men marching without food for four and five days and carrying the wounded through the curving and sloping mountain roads. Hiding my tears, I encouraged the ones with weak will to march on.

"The wounded could not be given adequate medical treatment because of the lack of medical supplies. There wasn't a one who did not have maggots on his wounds. The swinging motions of litters during the march, the fatigue, and excess loss of blood were too much for the patients and many died."

What went wrong? Lieutenant Hisatomi understood, if some of his superiors didn't. "Due to insufficient reconnaissance, the enemy situation and terrain were unknown," he said. "The deployment of the inner force into the jungle was difficult and the command of the troops at night could not be held securely. We completed preparations against enemy guns, but suffered heavy casualties before contact with the enemy's front line. There is a need for thorough study before jungle night attacks.

"Advancing without a single shot from our guns and heavy weapons is almost impossible. . . . It was pitiful."

Part of the problem was the Seventeenth Army's order of battle. As envisioned in planning in early August, the main fighting units were to be the Second and Thirty-eighth Divisions, the Kawaguchi Brigade (from the Eighteenth Division), the Ichiki Detachment (from the Twenty-eighth Regiment), the Fifth Tank Regiment, and the First Independent Tank Company.

But with these units came a bewildering array of supporting units— almost thirty of them, by our count. They included ten field artillery units and three anti-aircraft outfits. Service units included the likes of the Twenty-fourth Water Supply and Purification Unit, the Eightieth Telegraph Platoon, the Forty-second and Forty-fifth Fixed Radio units, and the Thirty-ninth Field Road Construction Unit.

The Japanese army was still basically designed for operations against the Chinese. Rather than make special divisions heavy in firepower for action against the more powerfully armed American units the Japanese preferred a more flexible system of assigning special units as needed. The result was that the Japanese on Guadalcanal lacked cohesion, especially when it came to providing artillery fire, either in support of their own advancing troops or in attempting to put Henderson Field out of operation.

Our artillery was integrated into each of our divisions. For most of the time, supporting fire on Guadalcanal came from Pedro del Valle's Eleventh Marines, and it was brilliantly executed. But we shouldn't forget the role of American warplanes in the campaign. The Japanese diaries refer again and again to the attacks from the air, some of which were deadly, most of which were disruptive, and all of which led to sagging Japanese morale. The Marines had their own air arm, and on Guadalcanal these aircraft were directed by Brigadier General Roy S. Geiger, who had graduated from the same officer training class as his friend Archer Vandegrift. Historian Richard Frank wrote that Geiger "understood to his bones that Marine aviation existed to support the riflemen, and he made it a point to visit the front lines periodically." Roy Geiger and his pilots in their Wildcat fighters and Dauntless dive-bombers (plus the Navy and Army Air Corps pilots who flew at their side) were heroes on Guadalcanal.

Why the Japanese didn't use their big guns more effectively to shut down Henderson Field and Geiger's aircraft remains one of the great mysteries of Guadalcanal. We have already pointed out that the Japanese didn't have to capture the field to destroy it, they simply had to render it unusable. But all they did was harass us with intermittent artillery fire. Colonel Cates worried all through the campaign that the Japanese would haul some big guns and ammunition up "the rugged and rocky slopes" of Mt. Austen and open fire on our positions, including the airfield. But they never did, and Cates said it is simply "unexplainable."

It had been standard practice in Western armies to fire guns en masse rather than singly. If guns are grouped, the impact of their shells landing on the target can be a shattering experience. This, of course, is what we did, again and again, at massed Japanese infantry. "I have always stressed the fact that steel is cheaper than flesh," Colonel Cates wrote in his memoir, in words that would no longer be considered politically correct. "So, as long as we have the ammunition, we will kick the tail-gate out and pour it in on them. The more 'Banzais!' the more bullets the bastards get. Yelling won't win this war."

The division's official report was somewhat less bloodthirsty in tone, but the message was the same. "To preserve direction [the Japanese] followed the conventional practice of moving dense columns of infantry along terrain lines leading to the objective." This allowed our artillery to cut them to pieces.

The Japanese seemed unable to grasp the importance of firepower in modern warfare. They fired their shells just a few at a time, and it is one reason why our casualties were as low as they were. The lack of effective artillery support is a standard gripe in almost all of the captured Japanese diaries.

We go back again to the spiritual dimension. Many Japanese officers still believed in the code named for an early Japanese warrior, Bushido, in which Japanese fighting spirit would overcome all opposition, even 75mm artillery shells. The skilled Japanese admiral, Tanaka, the victor in the battle of Tassafaronga, saw this for the twentieth-century nonsense that it was and commented after Ichiki's Detachment had been wiped out: "This tragedy should have taught the hopelessness of 'bamboo spear' tactics." It should have, but it didn't.

Part of the warrior code involved ritual suicide when the ebb and flow of battle turned against the Japanese. By doing so, these active and experienced officers simply did their enemy's work for them. By the same token, the individual Japanese soldier typically was willing to die for his emperor and his country in what seemed to us to be foolhardy attacks.

In a captured diary—probably from a soldier in the Thirty-eighth Division—we found this passage:

November 8: Last night's bombing was really fierce and just as terrifying. In fact all the news I hear worries me. It seems as if we have suffered considerable damage and casualties. They might be exaggerated, but it is pitiful. Far away from our home country, here on an isolated island, a fearful battle is raging. What these soldiers say is something of the supernatural and cannot be believed as human stories. However it is very reassuring to hear these soldiers say, "We must win, no matter what hardships we encounter; we must go forth with the firm conviction of ultimate victory." Yes, I too will die on this island as a guardian of the Emperor. Our regiment commander, battalion commander and many other comrades have died. I assure you that I will avenge them and I will pray for their peaceful heavenly bliss. Day has broken on this isolated island where thousands of the spirits of the departed heroes sleep. The world is created from destruction, and peace is acquired through war. Thus the world's history repeats itself.

To live to fight another day should be a soldier's guiding principle, we believed, but it wasn't an acceptable notion for many of these brave men.

The Japanese underestimated our military power. But, from the start of the campaign, they also believed our morale was sagging. A captured Japanese intelligence dispatch, dated August 14, said: "The enemy landing strength seems to be unexpectedly small . . . not only are they not using the airfield, but their activities are not vigorous." Wrong on all counts. We had landed in strength, and we were vigorously active, especially in preparing the airfield. We had a lot to learn about combat intelligence on Guadalcanal, but the Japanese were even less skilled.

Guadalcanal was not the American Navy's finest hour, despite the heroism of so many sailors and officers. If the Japanese night-fighting skills on land had been greatly exaggerated, there was nothing exaggerated about their night-fighting abilities at sea. Even with superior radar, the U.S. Navy sometimes proved inept in meeting the enemy. We simply hadn't prepared for this kind of fighting, though our admirals knew the Japanese preferred night actions. A key part of the Navy's problem at this stage in the war was ineffective leadership. Sometimes, the Marines believed, Admiral Turner served the Japanese better than he did the beleaguered troops ashore. Ghormley was in over his head, and the Navy only turned itself around when he was replaced by Halsey.

Good as the Japanese navy was around Guadalcanal, it exhibited the same shortcoming as the Japanese officers ashore—an inability to push home an advantage when it opened up to them. Even Mikawa, with his brilliant victory at Savo Island early in August, displayed this recurring weakness. With victory in hand, Mikawa could easily have destroyed all the defenseless American transports, and maybe ended the Marines' Guadalcanal campaign right then and there. But he hesitated, and then withdrew, an incredibly lucky break for our side.

It happened again that terrible night of October 11, when two Japanese battleships opened fire and destroyed most of our planes on Henderson Field. It was at this point, I told my students at Quantico, that the enemy was close, once again, to victory. But they failed to take full advantage of their formidable naval forces. Why, I asked, didn't they commit the two greatest battleships in the world, *Yamato* and *Musachi,* to the Guadalcanal operation? They sailed all over the South China Sea but never came close to us. The top Japanese admiral was Isoroku Yamamoto, and we still don't really know why he declined to commit more of his forces to the seven sea battles around Guadalcanal. Historians guess it may have been because the Japanese defeat at Midway made him wary.

We owed much of our success to our commanding general, Archer Vandegrift. He outfought and outthought his enemy throughout the campaign, and remained a reasonable and decent man from start to finish. Generally, once Vandegrift had the men he wanted in place, we were commanded by able, dedicated officers. But, still, there was "Wild Bill" McKelvy, just a little intoxicated, just a little confused, always impossibly difficult. For all that, McKelvy achieved results when he had to. We didn't miss him when he went home, but we will always remember him. He never commanded troops in battle again, and when he retired from the Marines in 1948, they promoted him to brigadier general.

And, on the Japanese side, the officer I will always remember was that curious little figure, Akinosuku Oka, whose performance on Guadalcanal flies in the face of everything we had been told about officers in the Japanese army.

Even the Japanese realized all was not well with Oka. Here's a diary entry from an unidentified Japanese officer dated October 26: "Last night, the night attack of the Third Battalion did not progress as we wished. They say that the Oka unit did not attack the enemy upon the order, and he (Oka) left his unit and stayed at this point 2 kilometers east of the narrow bridge. It seems that the regimental command does not know what to do with him."

I lectured about Oka, and I wrote about him in a series of articles in the *Marine Corps Gazette* in the summer of 1945, as the war drew to a close. An illustration in the magazine shows this fat little officer, clutching his helmet, spyglasses flying, running for his life. Nothing about Guadalcanal surprised me more than the discovery that one of the principal Japanese commanders was, of all unlikely things, a poltroon.

12

Thereafter

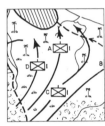

I was separated from the Marine Corps on January 5, 1945. Captain William Hollingsworth Whyte III, Retired.

What now? After more than four years in the Marines, I didn't intend to reenlist in the Vick School of Applied Merchandising. As far as I could tell, I had no marketable skills. But, in those days I spent teaching at Quantico, I had picked up a taste for writing. I had written seven pieces for the *Marine Corps Gazette,* the Marines' professional magazine.

Armed with my clippings, I applied for a job at *Fortune* magazine. For reasons known only to management, they took me on as an apprentice, at seventy-five dollars a week. I realized after a few days on the job that I was the worst writer on a staff that included such professionals as Eric Hodges, Walker Evans, and Herbert Solow, to name just a few. They were helpful but exasperated. My greatest weakness was an inability to come up with a theme to give unity to whatever I was writing.

One editor was particularly harsh. "Whyte," he said, "you should go back to that town of yours—East Chester, or whatever it's called. You're not gonna make it here, kid."

But in setting off on a writing career, my knowledge of maps and my experience on Guadalcanal ultimately saved the day. It was in drawing those maps that I had learned to look at things carefully. Most people don't do that. My strength has been the simple ability to see things other people have missed. I was trained to do that by the United States Marine Corps.

We had to look at things carefully on Guadalcanal, because our lives depended on it. In one of those articles in the *Marine Corps Gazette* I said that "our men's powers of observation deteriorated rapidly after 15 minutes, *when there was no activity to be seen.*" But when something suspicious was observed, "not only the observer but all hands turned to watching the suspect area, their interest aroused at being finally able to observe something other than the fluttering about of white cockatoos."

It takes great patience to observe things accurately. In that same article in the *Gazette,* I recalled that one of our outposts reported a "group of enemy digging in" at a spot we had been routinely observing. More careful scrutiny revealed that the "enemy" was a herd of native cattle. "Since the moving objects had been in hostile territory, the observer felt justified in assuming they were enemy. Nip this sort of thing in the bud by practical exercises in observation to show the men how misleading both their senses and their memories can be," I wrote.

If it's important to look carefully, it's just as important to listen attentively. In my standard lecture at Quantico, I challenged the students this way:

Gentlemen, one object of this lesson is to demonstrate to you how much keener your senses are than you realize, and how important this is to you. We're going to have an experiment.

In the record I am going to play for you, there are roughly 32 well-known American slang phrases that the Japanese soldiers are taught to fool the Americans. "Hi, hi, hi, hi, hi," is one of them. Others are, "Marine, you die," or, "Eleanor [Roosevelt], you die."

I'm going to turn off the lights to let you concentrate while I play the record, and when I turn them on again and ask for a show of hands, only raise your hands for phrases that are clearly identifiable. OK, gentlemen.

(Lights off. Record plays. Lights back on again.)

Hausknecht, how many did you hear? Nine? Colonel, how about you? Eleven.

It was a dirty trick, of course. There were no American phrases, slang or otherwise, on the recording. My purpose simply was to hammer home a common human frailty: we see what we want to see and we hear what we want to hear.

In my initial efforts at *Fortune* I didn't have much chance to use the powers of observation I had developed in the blueberry patches of Cape Cod and the jungles of Guadalcanal. But I began to show a modest flair for my new career in my first major piece for *Fortune*—a story about the college "Class of 1949."

Managing editor Del Paine had called me into his office—my first appearance there—and said maybe I would be interested in doing a story no one else on the staff wanted to take on. It was a story, he said, about one of the finest college classes to come out of Yale University, ever, and the source for this claim was Yale's president, Whitney Griswold.

I decided to make a rudimentary check of campuses around the country, and my first interviews were somewhat alarming. It was all very well for Griswold to say how great his graduating Yalies were, but the situation at other colleges didn't seem nearly so promising. Griswold's Yalies weren't great enough on their own to sustain a piece in *Fortune* magazine.

So I continued to talk to people—listening, without prejudice—to what these members of the Class of '49 were saying, and I confirmed my original impression. This class, at Yale and everywhere else, wasn't all that hot. Most amazing, seniors, almost to a man (or woman), were rejecting the old Protestant, entrepreneurial ethic. These young people weren't seeking excitement, or challenge. They wanted a safe haven. They wanted to work for AT&T and General Electric, for heaven's sake!

The story was just the opposite of what we had expected. It made for a shocking piece—shocking, that is, to that generation who still believed in rugged individualism. This was man bites dog, and it clinched my job at *Fortune*. I had done what I had been preaching—I had observed carefully and listened attentively, and all the while I had kept my mind open to the possibility that the famous president of Yale University might be wrong.

All of this reporting led, inevitably, to my book *The Organization Man*, published in 1956. In that book, I pointed out how pervasive the organization had become in the lives of millions of Americans. "The fault," I wrote, "is not in organization, it is in our worship of it." I said there must always be a conflict between the individual and society, "and it is the price of being an individual that he must face these conflicts. He cannot evade them, and in seeking an ethic that offers a spurious peace of mind, thus does he tyrannize himself."

A good part of the book is essentially reportorial—chapters in which I attempted to show the organization man (this, remember, was the mid-1950s, pretty much pre-organization woman) at work, at home, at play, at rest. And, you bet, I used maps in every conceivable way. I couldn't have written Part VII (The New Suburbia) without them.

When we examined these suburban communities, we charted New Year's Eve parties, coffee parties, Tuesday-afternoon bridge clubs. We plotted the rate of turnover in each subdivision, the concentration of budding civic leaders. We mapped it all, and my maps revealed fascinating patterns that couldn't be attributed to chance.

I left *Fortune* in 1958 to pursue my growing interest in the environment and open spaces, and, most particularly, the great potential of something called an easement. I was supported in this new line of work by Laurance S. Rockefeller.

An easement is one of many parts of the bundle of rights that is land ownership. Any one of these rights can be transferred by an easement to another party. They can be given away or sold, to an individual or to an institution. Easements "run with the land" and are binding on successive owners.

In preserving open space, easements work. The owner of the land deserving to be preserved as open space simply sells—or, better yet, gives away—by easement his right to develop that land. It was a tough sell at first, but in time we were able to pass easement legislation in a number of states, including Pennsylvania, New York, and California. Easements remain a useful device in land planning.

But what about the way the land not under easements or any other restrictions was being filled in by sprawling housing developments? In the early 1950s, everyone said population density was what was wrong with our big urban centers. Too many people jammed into too little space. But high density wasn't the culprit. It had been demonstrated that the more people who jam the streets and the neighborhoods, the more vibrant—and safe—the neighborhood is for everybody.

In the suburbs, we had these little lots filled up with Cape Cods, ranches, and Hansels and Gretels, gobbling up land at a prodigious rate. Why couldn't we bring the density principle to the suburbs? we asked. Backed by the American Conservation Association, we came up with an ancient concept—grouping houses closely together and using the land we saved to create common greens and squares. We called it cluster development. And it worked, too. What we found was that people like to live in these open-space developments, once they get used to watching their children play near streams, valleys, and woods.

Once again, it was a simple idea, growing out of the way we observed land patterns. Good maps were a major part of it.

But I suppose nothing I have done demonstrates the lessons I learned on Guadalcanal as much as the Street Life Project, initiated in New York City in 1970.

It took off following one of those street conversations we would, in time, study with such intensity. One day I was walking down Madison Avenue when I bumped into an old friend, Conrad Wirth, director of the National Park Service and a member of the National Geographic Society's board. We stopped to chat. After the usual pleasantries, he asked me if I could use some money to support my research project on street life. Yes, indeed, I said, I certainly could. "How much do you think would be right?" he asked. With a deep breath I said $25,000. "Make it $35,000," he replied. The transaction was repeated the following year, and so it was that I was the first person to receive an "expedition grant" from the National Geographic Society.

My book on this research, *City: Rediscovering the Center,* published in 1988, begins: "For the past sixteen years I have been walking the streets and public spaces of the city and watching how people use them." Scouting, you might say. Patrolling.

"The city is full of vexations," I wrote, but simple observation of street patterns—and maps to back us up—showed how we could correct many of these irksome problems. Steps are too steep. Doors are too tough to open. Ledges are so high or so low you can't sit on them, and when they are at the right height, somebody has put spikes on them to keep "undesirables" away.

And those terrible blank walls. Nothing irritates me more. According to my computations, the proportion of downtown block fronts that are blank at street level has been growing rapidly, mostly in small cities, which are the ones most immediately hurt by suburban shopping malls and most tempted to combat their tormentors by copying them.

What we need most are busy, lively streets. The street is the river of life of the city, the place where we come together, the pathway to the center. Using time-lapse photography, we charted pedestrian movement on these busy streets. I was curious about the way pedestrians used the sidewalks for conversations. I presumed these people would move out of the traffic flow of hundreds of other in-a-hurry people to have these conversations. Not so. The great bulk of the conversations took place smack in the middle of the flow—what I called the 100 percent location.

We put a lot of what we had discovered together in another project, restoring Bryant Park. We found ways to clear this beautiful space of the drug dealers who had taken it over; we gave it back to the people of New York. For the first time in a century, Bryant Park works. I can prove it. I have maps—*accurate* maps—showing what we accomplished.

Appendix A

Hyakutake Meets the Marines[1]
Captain William H. Whyte, Jr.

On the night of October 17, 1942, an expectant buzz ran through the group of soldiers gathered by the beach at the little native village of Kokumbona on the north coast of Guadalcanal, for in the party of officers that had just come ashore was none other than Lt. General Haruyoshi Hyakutake—commander of the Imperial Seventeenth Army, the spearhead to Nippon's invincible drive to Australia and New Zealand.

After being greeted with much bowing and scraping by an official welcoming party, the heavily beribboned general and his top staff officers went immediately to the luxurious tent of Lt. General Maruyama, commander of the Second Division. They listened carefully as Hyakutake's Chief of Intelligence, Lt. Colonel Matsumoto, outlined the situation of the beleaguered Yankees at Lunga Point. Last minute changes were made in the plans—plans that had been prepared at Rabaul with all of the cunning and deception for which Hyakutake was famed.

They were now chattering happily over their cups of warm sake, for no longer were they to suffer humiliation at the hands of the American devils. The shoe was on the other foot, for in the last two weeks the tide had turned with amazing suddenness. The great Admiral Yamamoto himself had come down to direct the final phase of the naval struggle; already units of his mighty Combined Fleet had shelled the enemy positions in a series of brutal night bombardments. The bulk of the Naval Air Force was gathered at Rabaul, and, perhaps what was most important, the newly arrived 150-mm howitzers had begun shelling the American airfield at Lunga Point. At last, after many bitter setbacks, the full might of the Seventeenth Army was deployed for the final blow, and among the hundreds of little groups of soldiers huddled around their rice fires from Visale to Point Cruz there was new hope.

It was a strange island they had come to, stretching east and west some 90 miles, with a spiny backbone of precipitous mountains that rose as high as 8,000 feet. Along the center of the north coast the mountains lowered to give way to a series of coastal coconut plantations and large kunai grass plains interspersed with countless rivers and streams. But towards the western end of the north coast the plains gave way to a weird labyrinth of sharp, grass covered coral ridges, the ravines between them choked with dense vegetation and 150-foot high dilo and banyan trees. Though the soldiers had often cursed the mud, the flies, the mosquitoes, the land crabs, and the oppressive heat, they had given their thanks to the sharpness of those ridges that had protected them so well from the fierce American artillery fire, and likewise to the jungle canopy that had concealed them from enemy dive bombers.

From these same ridges they could see the whole arena of battle from one spot—to the east the American positions on the delta of the Lunga River; to the west, the rugged Cape Esperance, and across from it, tiny Savo Island. Twenty miles to the north, easily visible on a good day was the island of Florida, with its satellite isles of Tulagi, Gavutu, and Tanambogo.

Formerly all of these islands had been under British rule, but in the early months of the war the enemy had only been able to maintain a small seaplane base at Tulagi and a few scattered garrisons elsewhere. Admiral Yamamoto had long realized the potentialities of this area as a naval and air base from which to stage the invasion of Port Moresby and the subsequent drive to Australia and New Zealand. As soon as Rabaul was secured, he sent down the Kure 3d Special Naval Landing Force to seize Tulagi. It fell like a ripe plum on May 3d and soon base units began pouring in.

Curiously enough it wasn't until July 1, long after the Japanese "victory" in the Coral Sea necessitated postponement of the Port Moresby operation that Guadalcanal itself was occupied, but the plans for utilizing its large grassy plains had been well laid. Aerial photos had revealed the Lunga Point area as perhaps the best potential airbase site. Accordingly when Captain Kodama and Lt. Commander Okimura arrived there with their two Naval Construction battalions, they at once began work clearing an airstrip.

Having liberated the natives from the evils of British imperialism Captain Kodama proceeded to make known the benefits of membership in the Greater East Asia Co-Prosperity Sphere. Every native was to be an "Applicant for forced labor." The labor was to consist of a month's work on the airfield; working hours 0500 until 1700 daily, pay figured at one stick of tobacco per week, and a loin cloth at the end of the month. For those who worked well Capt. Kodama promised a handsome good conduct badge, and as an extra inducement natives whose work was particularly diligent might be made a chief, with several "little chiefs" to boss.

An Object Lesson by Ishimoto

Melanesian enthusiasm for work, never very strong under any circumstances, was so notably absent that despite threats and reprisals there was soon hardly a native to be found in the area. In addition there were disquieting rumors that a larger native army of 1,000 men was operating along the eastern end of the north coast under the direction of several English adventurers. Although this report seemed an exaggeration, there was a good bit of mopping up to be done. Along with the force was just the man for this sort of work—Ishimoto.

For several long years Ishimoto had endured the patronizing airs of his English masters as he worked at his ostensible trade of carpentry at Tulagi and Guadalcanal. Now, returning with the victorious Imperial Forces, he could hardly wait to greet his old enemies in his naval uniform. No longer would he have to bow and hiss politely at their reprimands, no longer would he live like a slave. He would teach these dogs a lesson!

With a group of 40-odd Naval Landing Troops from Tulagi he began scouring the villages along the north coast of Guadalcanal. He went after the troublemakers first—the missionaries. None of these hypocrites had fled, but had instead remained at their missions. On being questioned they brazenly claimed that they were not communicating with the English, but instead were looking after the needs of their "flock." Some of the other mopping up patrols merely requisitioned their supplies and personal belongings, but Ishimoto was not so easily to be misled. He knew the hold they had on childish natives, and although there was no proof, he was sure they were up to no good.

The Catholic mission near Tasimboko was the worst offender, for the priest and the three nuns there took little pains to disguise their dislike for him. At first Ishimoto had only intended to threaten them, but the priest's insolent manner, his lying answers when interrogated, demanded stronger measures. The whole thing broke when one of the nuns, evidently frightened by the playful gestures directed at them by the men, suddenly ran into the bush. They couldn't catch her, but the other two nuns and the priest were quickly tied to the coconut trees in front of the mission. Maddened by the insane sobbing of the women, and with the warmth of the sake stirring in him all of the memories of former insults, Ishimoto's patience broke. With a cry of anger he seized a rifle from one of the men and plunged its bayonet into the priest's belly. Screaming and yelling with excitement the men rushed to do the same to the nuns. After the execution was over Ishimoto decided to leave the disemboweled bodies as they were as a lesson to the natives.

There was still a good bit of unfinished business to do, as the Englishman Clemens, former district officer of the island, was still at large. He had to be caught, for the base radio at Tulagi was intercepting suspicious coded messages coming from a transmitter somewhere on Guadalcanal. At first it seemed as if it would be an easy task but the natives refused to cooperate. Whenever a Japanese patrol entered a native village, most of the natives were nowhere be found. If they did appear they either pretended they could not understand the Japs' pidgin English or else claimed they knew nothing of Clemens. Once a cooperative native told them of the Englishman's whereabouts, but by the time the patrol had reached the spot Clemens, evidently forewarned by his native scouts, had fled.

Despite the defection of the native workers, by the middle of July things were humming. At the finger wharves at Kukum ships were busy unloading vast quantities of aviation equipment, food, and post exchange supplies, including 125,000 pounds of rice, dried kelp, canned goods, cider, beer, and sake. Neat tent cities were erected, complete with electric lights, giant refrigerators, reinforced air raid shelters, and elaborate concrete privies. The airfield was coming along well and would in a few weeks be ready for the planes at Rabaul.

It was just too easy. Here was being completed a base which would soon be the springboard for the decisive operations against the islands to the east and the U. S.—Australia supply route, and yet, save for several insignificant raids by B-17s, there was no enemy interference. Little wonder that Radio Tokyo jibed, "Where are the United States Marines? The Marines are supposed to be the finest soldiers in the world—but no one has seen them!"

It was a very surprised Captain Kodama who was awakened the morning of August 7 by shells from a large American fleet standing offshore and by the dive bombing of scores of carrier based planes. Utter confusion reigned throughout the camp, with everyone running this way and that. The workers, low class men anyway, were hopeless, and fled in any direction they could. But Captain Kodama, although shaken by this unfortunate event, was nobody's fool and soon realized that this was just another one of the American's hit and run raids. As there was no sense in standing around in this maelstrom, he ordered the troops to withdraw to the safety of the jungle ravines to the west. When the enemy fleet had fled or been annihilated, everyone would return to Lunga Point.

No sooner, however, had the troops reached the Matanikau River when Captain Kodama saw to his horror that the Americans were approaching Lunga Point in landing barges! How in the world to explain this to Headquarters at Rabaul? He finally managed to compose a dispatch chronicling a heroic fight in which his command had been pushed westward by overwhelming numbers.

This news created consternation at Rabaul, but after several hours' reflection the commanders began to wonder if perhaps the Yankees had not played into their hands. A powerful cruiser task force was immediately assembled and ordered to catch the American fleet while it was immobilized for the protection of the transports. With great skill and cunning the Japanese commander slipped down under the cover of darkness and found the American fleet lying unsuspectingly off Savo Island. Within a few moments it was all but annihilated, even the Americans later admitting the loss of four heavy cruisers.

But despite the glorious naval victory it was necessary to organize a ground force to retake Guadalcanal—the reduction of Tulagi to follow later. This task was given to Lt. General Hyakutake's Seventeenth Army.

Now actually the Seventeenth Army had been formed for quite another task—the invasion of Southeastern New Guinea—and while the headquarters was now at Rabaul its units had still not yet been completely gathered together. Speed was essential, however, so Hyakutake had to do some quick improvising.

A Powerhouse Force on Paper
His Army consisted chiefly of the Second and Thirty-eighth infantry divisions, an independent regiment, and a brigade, heavily supported by one mountain and two heavy field artillery regiments, three AA, two anti-

tank, and two mortar battalions, plus the usual service units—field hospitals, stevedore companies, engineer regiments, and so on.

It was a powerhouse force—on paper. By later October the bulk of it could be concentrated, but Hyakutake couldn't wait until then to commence operations. Homeward bound from Guam, however, was a unit assigned to him—Colonel Kiyono Ichiki's crack 28th Regiment. This shock outfit had been marking time in the Central Pacific for several months as one of the assault units of the "Midway Occupation Force," and now, regrettable circumstances having forced the dissolution of that task force, it was on its way back to Tokyo. Hyakutake wired Ichiki to put about immediately and head for Truk, orders to follow later.

There were several things Ichiki's 2,500 men could do before the arrival of other units; they could stage raids on the American positions; conduct extensive guerrilla type operations, or they could move about outside the enemy perimeter lobbing mortar and artillery shells onto the airfield.

While it was estimated that as many as 10,000 Americans had landed at Lunga Point, there was evidence that morale was low. For one thing, their attack on Lunga Point had seemed extremely cautious, for they would not advance without the most heavy preparatory fires. They were not yet using the airfield, although it was virtually finished, and every night the Japanese troops grinned as they listened to the Americans fire prodigious quantities of ammunition into the night air. Truly, they were a spineless lot.

Despite the fact that Americans had heavy numerical superiority, the proven qualitative superiority of the Jap fighting man led Hyakutake to decide to give Ichiki a free hand, and to let him land and attack the airfield as soon as possible, rather than stage small scale harassing actions.

By August 15, the unit had arrived at Truk, and Ichiki, delighted with Hyakutake's order, had completed his plan. Because of transportation difficulties, he split his force into two echelons. The first, consisting of 900 men and himself, was to embark in destroyers and land between Taivu and Koli Points the night of August 17, then to march on Lunga Point, attack and seize the airfield in one surprise blow. When the second echelon landed on the 24th they would have the job of mopping up.

At 2100 of the 17th the entire first echelon landed from the destroyers in rubber boats, and by morning were all set for the advance to the west.

When Ishimoto arrived at Ichiki's command post he had little valuable information to offer, despite the fact that he had been patrolling the north coast for many weeks. It was certain, however, that the Yankees had been able to enlist some of the natives as spies. Only a few days before, Ishimoto told Ichiki, his old enemy, Vouza, a Sergeant Major in the native police force, had brazenly walked into his bivouac. On being questioned Vouza denied that he knew anything of the Americans' activities. Ishimoto, suspicious, had him searched. An angry shout went up from the men as one of them unrolled a piece of cloth that had been hidden under Vouza's lava-lava. It was a tiny American flag! Ishimoto commanded the men to tie him to a tree. A little bayonet practice would loosen his tongue!

It was maddening. Hour after hour Ishimoto bellowed and shouted at Vouza as the men sliced at his jet black skin with their bayonets. The black native would not say a word. When dusk came he had lapsed into unconsciousness and was dying.

It was most unfortunate, however, Ishimoto explained to Ichiki, but the next morning there was no trace of Vouza. It was incredible that he had lived through the interrogation but the fact had to be faced that he had probably made his way to the Marine lines.

Despite the fact that radio communication from his advance patrol had stopped suddenly, Ichiki's forward elements reached the mouth of the Tenaru River the night of the 20th. It was here the Americans had their easternmost positions strung out along the west bank of the sluggish lagoon-like river. Seeing that the key to the position was the narrow sandspit across the mouth, Ichiki planned to build a base of fire with his 70-mm battalion guns, heavy machineguns, and grenade dischargers in the coconut grove on the east bank, while his massed infantry would in a sudden shock attack surge across the sandspit.

After a short but violent preparation, the men screaming and yelling at the top of their lungs rushed across the sandspit. The Americans reeled back, and a bridgehead was quickly secured on the west bank. But the enemy resistance was unexpectedly fierce—Americans who had been encircled stuck to their guns, and others—fierce, huge bearded men—rushed forward in hand to hand combat. By dawn the Americans were grinding the Japs back across the spit, and artillery and mortar fire was increasing in intensity.

Following Through on a Decision

Ichiki now found that his initial assault had been repulsed and that his left flank was completely exposed. But Ichiki had made his decision and would let no fortunes of the moment dismay him. He ordered one of his companies to advance through the surf and swoop in on the American left flank from the sea. The long hours of training in such tactics for the Midway operation were now to bear fruit.

Skillfully the men pushed through the water until they were opposite the American beach positions, then, screaming and yelling, they clambered up onto the beach. They were met with canister fire from antitank guns. The carnage was terrible, and the flanking unit was quickly annihilated.

Five American tanks suddenly appeared on the other side of the river and dashed across the sandspit. Ichiki didn't have a single antitank gun to stop them, but his men rushed at them courageously with magnetic mines. The tanks made quick work of these men and they cruised back and forth machinegunning and running over the tightly packed soldiers.

Soon there was the sound of shots to the rear—the enemy had outflanked them! Ichiki quickly made the decision to burn the regimental colors—for above all else the Japanese code demanded that they never fall into the hands of the enemy. As the last remnants of his command were being slaughtered, Ichiki burnt the colors, and then, true to the code of Bushido, he and his adjutant committed suicide. By dark, save for the handful that had remained at Koli Point, there were no survivors.

Hyakutake had had infinite faith in the fighting powers of the Jap soldier, but he had not campaigned for years on the plains of China without attaining a certain flexibility which many of his more ardent subordinates lacked. He had had great hopes for the Ichiki Detachment—perhaps it would pull off a coup that would go down in history, but he was taking no chances. At the same time that he was wishing Ichiki luck in his mission he was meanwhile ordering another outfit, the Kawaguchi Brigade, to carry out precisely the same job—the seizure of the airfield—two weeks later.

Major General Kiyotake Kawaguchi's brigade had come to the Seventeenth Army fresh from it victorious campaign in Borneo, and at the time of the American landing on Guadalcanal was busy at Palau rehearsing the Port Moresby operation. It was immediately alerted, and as soon as the necessary transports were available, was rushed to the Shortland Islands. Here it had to unload into destroyers for final night runs down to Guadalcanal for at this time daylight landings were too difficult since the Americans had now finally begun to operate planes from the airfield at Lunga Point.

The brigade was composed of the 124th Regiment's three infantry battalions, an infantry battalion of another unit, and the now orphaned second echelon of the Ichiki Detachment, plus artillery, AA, and engineer units—a total force of about 5,000 men. Even before he had arrived on the island Kawaguchi had sketched out his basic plan. The 2nd Battalion of Colonel Akinosuke Oka's 124th Regiment would land under Oka himself near the Matanikau River to the west of the American positions, while the rest of the force landed, like the Ichiki unit, between Taivu and Koli Points.

There would be no rash advance this time, but rather a slow, steady secret movement through the jungle to the south of the enemy positions. Then, in one coordinated blow, Oka's force would hit the enemy from the west, while the real powerhouse punch would be delivered along a spiny ridge south of the airfield. The second echelon of the Ichiki Detachment was given the job of attacking across the Tenaru (further upstream this time) in order to put to rest the souls of Ichiki and his men.

By September 6, after an entire week of sneak night landings, the bulk of the outfit had been landed and was now assembled near the native village of Tasimboko, ready to begin the westward advance. Unfortunately, however, the Americans had discovered the landing place, and planes began to strafe and dive bomb them. The troops, who only a few days before, had been celebrating their forthcoming victory with an extra ration of one shot of sake per man, were now in a dismal state. It rained continuously—even worse than those torrential downpours they had hated so much in Borneo; the air raids never ceased, and to add insult to injury, a force of Yankees had insultingly landed on the 8th at Tasimboko and destroyed all of their AA guns, several field pieces, and huge quantities of rations. What made it irritating was that the enemy could easily have been wiped out had they dared to engage the main force bivouacked further west, but the only men guarding the supplies at Tasimboko had been the miserable service troops. These good for nothing soldiers, who constantly pilfered the front line fighters' food, had run at the first sight of the enemy.

While it appeared that the contents of four American transports had been landed in his rear at Taivu Point, Kawaguchi nevertheless determined to begin his westward advance and let his flanks and rear take care of themselves. It was a wise decision, for in a few days it became obvious that the American attack at Tasimboko had only been a raid and that the troops had since reembarked.

Kawaguchi had not expected his men to make particularly good time for he had ordered them to put secrecy above speed. Instead of walking across the wide grassy plains, the men had to cut and hack their way through the dense jungle bordering them. If the fields had to be crossed, it would only be at night and even then footprints werc to be obliterated. It was a slow, painful process, but the timetable that had been laid out was followed with amazing accuracy. There had been a few patrol clashes with the enemy, but it appeared that they had not suspected the trail was being cut so far to the south. By the 12th the units were in concealed positions south of the airfield ready for the attack.

The original plan still stood basically unchanged, save that a full strength battalion replaced the remnants of the Ichiki Detachment for the attack against the upper Tenaru. The attack of Oka's one battalion against the western flank and the attack of the main force south of the airfield would jump off at 2000 of the 13th, while two hours later the 1st Battalion of the 124th Regiment would hit the American east flank at the upper Tenaru.

The Navy and Air Force stepped up their pounding of the enemy positions to prepare them for Kawaguchi's attack. At noon of the 12th, 27 bombers escorted by several fighter squadrons pasted the airfield. At midnight two cruisers and four destroyers began shelling Lunga Point and kept it up for three and a half hours. The 13th saw practically every bomber at Rabaul thrown into the preparation with formations blasting the Americans about every three hours.

The Americans knew something was up for their patrols were blindly stabbing out in all directions. Several strong ones had bumped into the main force south of the airfield the night of the 12th but had been pushed back without too much trouble. Over in the east, where Major Ishitari's 1st battalion 124th lay waiting concealed in the jungle beside a large grassy field, the Yankee reconnaissance efforts were laughable. One 30-man enemy patrol stumbled out into the field at noon of the 13th and became so engrossed with eating their rations and watching the dog fights overhead that they failed to notice that more than 900 rifles were aimed at them. The temptation to annihilate these stupid "lookout" troops was great, but Major Ishitari, realizing that secrecy was more important than the killing of a few enemy, ordered that no one shoot. To his amazement he saw the Americans were now walking along the edge of the field right towards his battalion's secret bivouac. They ambled along smoking and chattering away with hardly so much as a glance at their flanks or rear, and although Ishitari could almost reach out and touch them, they passed by in blissful ignorance of their peril. The men were quite put out that they had not been allowed to take several Yankees alive for "questioning" and kill the rest, but their officers pointed out that this incident meant they would take the enemy completely by surprise that night.

As soon as dusk fell the battalion started wading down the Ilu River single file. At 2000 the head of the column reached a bend in the river where they were to turn west and begin the attack across the open plain in front of the American positions. A small group of enemy lying in ambush opened fire on them, but scattered as the men began to surround them. No sooner had the enemy outpost been annihilated than a terrific burst of firing and yelling met them from another force 100 yards down the river from them. For 15 minutes the firing grew hotter and hotter as the two forces battled it out. Major Ishitari, however, began to notice a strange similarity between the sounds of his own men's yells and those of the enemy unit. Perhaps the Americans had learned some Japanese phrases . . . or it could be that . . . ? Ishitari screamed at the top of his lungs for his men to cease fire, then yelling in the direction of the other force proclaimed his identity. There was sudden silence as all firing stopped, then a quavering voice from the other force informed him that he had been battling one of his own companies that had taken a short cut. Had there not been more pressing affairs Ishitari would have seen to it that the stupid dunce of a company commander understood he had to kill himself for this inexcusable blunder.

But H-hour had already passed so Ishitari hurriedly realigned his companies while the advance unit sneaked through the high grass to cut the enemy barbed wire. When the sound of enemy machinegun fire told him that the advance party had done its work Ishitari ordered his companies to attack. Before they could go more than a few feet there was a terrible roar as a terrific artillery barrage whistled down on them. The attack had been stopped before the men could get near enough to the enemy for a charge—typical of the cowardly fashion in which the Americans hid behind material superiority rather than face Japanese bayonets.

The Emperor Is Served
The next morning the men dug their foxholes deeper as they prepared for a second night attack. One American, evidently a survivor of the outpost, was found hiding in the bushes by the river and was immediately bayo-

neted to death as he vainly tried to crawl away. There was one shameful incident, however, for two other Americans hiding in the bushes on the opposite side of the river only a few yards away from Major Ishitari's command post, suddenly jumped up in front of Privates Miyoko and Yamada. Although the Yankees were unarmed they were of such ferocious appearance that Miyoko and Yamada turned around and ran. Before anyone could stop them, the Yankees ran right through the lines into the tall grass and safety.

Everything was going wrong. Ishitari admitted it when he gathered his company commanders for a conference at noon. True, three American tanks that had cruised back and forth in front of the antitank guns had been knocked out, but it was apparent that casualties in the attack that night were going to be heavy. The only solace Ishitari could offer was that their sacrifice would serve the Emperor and their country.

If misfortune had struck before, catastrophe struck that night. The men bravely rushed to the attack, but the enemy artillery was unspeakably fierce. Within one hour 230 men, among them Ishitari, were killed, and 100 others were wounded so badly that when the retreat began, they had to be carried on litters.

Over on the ridge south of the airfield the main force's three battalions had launched their attack northward up the ridge leading to the airfield as scheduled. There didn't appear to be more than about 600–800 enemy troops holding the area and they had no barbed wire or pillboxes as there had been over by the Tenaru. It wasn't long before the enemy front line was overwhelmed and several units broke through to what appeared to be the American general's headquarters. Victory was almost in the bag, but the Americans were fighting with unusual ferocity, and gave ground only after the most bloody hand to hand fighting. By 0200 Kawaguchi's men had pushed the Americans back to the last ridge position protecting the airfield. The battle see-sawed back and forth for several hours, but try as they might, the Japanese could not break through. Casualties mounted to alarming proportions as the now consolidated enemy increased their fire. By morning it was obvious the attacks had failed.

Kawaguchi had listened in vain for the sound of firing from the west which would tell him of the attack of Colonel Oka and his battalion. Oka had preferred to keep his unit in comparative comfort down by the Matanikau River rather than go through the disagreeable task of hacking trails up to the American positions. His staff officers, who knew this pudgy, bombastic little man all too well, secretly suspected that he intended to put off his attack until the main push had been successful so that the going would be easy. After enough firing to justify its being called an attack, he called the whole thing off and retired once more to his hideout by the Matanikau. This disinclination of Oka's for real combat, although now disguised behind his strutting bravado, was to persist through later and more crucial actions.

Kawaguchi was meanwhile assembling the remnants of his shattered force for the retreat to the safety of the western ridges. The men, few of them unwounded, all of them hungry, were so dazed by the enormity of their failure that it all seemed like a bad dream. "We had never experienced this retreat march in the China Incident," wrote one officer to his wife, "but while our circumstances are indeed pathetic it is in many ways inspiring. The great heroes are not always found on the field of battle but also in the aftermath of defeat. The sight of these soldiers enduring hardships and hunger, their kindly affection and care for the wounded is even more beautiful than the picture of them in victory. These are the qualities of only the faithful and well trained armies. I cannot help from crying when I see the sight of these men marching without food or water for four or five days, and carrying the wounded through the curving and sloping mountain tracks of this terrible island. I have to hide my—there isn't a one without maggots in his wounds. The swinging motion of the litters during the march, the fatigue, and the excess loss of blood are too much . . . hundreds died."

The retreat had been an orderly one when it first started, but as the terrible march continued discipline began to vanish, and the force broke up into little groups.

The trail was over a succession of precipitous ridges, each one covered with dense undergrowth. The lead units, unencumbered with loads, didn't fare so badly, but the rear units, carrying the wounded on litters, and charged with bringing along the heavy weapons and ammunition, could barely make a mile a day. Almost everyone was suffering from malaria and dysentery. Men dropped by the trail constantly. Cremation was out of the question, and no one had the strength to dig graves, so the dead were left by the trail where they had fallen. Rations were completely gone except for what little rice each man had on him, and the cans of soy bean mash which a few of the luckier had kept. The rice had to be cooked, but enemy planes circled overhead constantly waiting for a wisp of smoke to reveal the location of the column. During the advance along the coast they had made smokeless fires from the husks of dried coconuts, but there was nothing in this dank jungle that would burn without giving off clouds of smoke. Only at night did they dare make fires, and even then they often found themselves where no water to boil the rice was to be had.

The jungle, formerly their ally, had now become hideous. During the day little sun pierced through the vault-like canopy of vines and creepers over head, but the damp heat was nonetheless stifling and the stench of rotting leaves overpowering. There were insects everywhere, and there wasn't a tree that wasn't swarming with thousands of red ants.

Just before dark the men would stop and clear out a place to spend the night. The wounded would be laid a distance down the trail so that the odor of their gangrenous wounds and their delirious cries wouldn't keep the others awake. With the undergrowth heavy with moisture there were no dry patches to sleep on. The night sounds of the jungle—the bark of the repulsive giant lizards, the mocking shrieks of the cockatoos—anyone of them a possible enemy signal, never seemed more frightening. Although the men were too tired to brush the mosquitos off their malaria wracked bodies they knew the deadly anopheles were at work.

The ordeal was terrible, but the spiritual fibre of the troops was equal to it. More maddening than the physical discomforts was the feeling of abandonment—the sense that their sacrifices were not known by those in the homeland. On the night of the 18th Kawaguchi's headquarters unit, resting in a small ravine at the base of Mt. Austen, heard over the short wave radio a broadcast of a patriotic mass meeting in Hinomiya Stadium in Tokyo. The moaning of their wounded was drowned out temporarily as they heard the voice of Captain Hiraide, Imperial Navy spokesman, proclaim exultantly, "The Marines left in the lurch have been faring miserably since they were the victim of Roosevelt's gesture . . . (Cheers) the stranded 10,000 have since been practically wiped out." It was embarrassing to listen to him go on to explain that so truthful were the Imperial communiques that the bulk of the American people had turned to them to get the real facts. The next night was just as bad, for a General Staff commentator in his radio analysis of the news stated ". . . approximately 10,000 Marines walked into a Japanese trap and were annihilated when the Japanese adopted 'drawing-in' tactics by leaving a small decoy force in the Solomon Islands."

But if nothing else had been accomplished in this terrible defeat, at least it had stirred up the high command to a realization of the gravity of the situation. By the time that the remnants of the Kawaguchi Brigade were reaching the Matanikau, the first groups of the main force of the Seventeenth Army were landing and Admiral Yamamoto's Combined Fleet was massing at Truk. It would be different this time, for General Hyakutake was coming down himself to direct the decisive operation, and he had a plan that couldn't fail.

Conclusion

The over-confidence had sobered the planning officers, who knew now that annihilating Americans would be difficult. There was the Matanikau River barrier to be secured. Even up at Rabaul, with only photographs to look at, Hyakutake had realized that a vital preliminary to the big offensive was a firm grasp on the sandspit at the river mouth. While it seemed doubtful that the Americans would leave the safety of their defense positions, Hyakutake was canny enough to recognize the importance of the river.

Why so important? The narrow river was not fordable, and the banks were lined with ridges so precipitous that virtually the only spot at which heavy equipment could be transported was over the sandspit running across the mouth. Since the big drive depended so much on getting across tanks and heavy artillery now being landed, Hyakutake ordered his Second Division commander, LtGen Masao Maruyama, to see to it that a fresh regiment defend the vital east bank.

When Maruyama arrived the first week in October with the first part of his Second Division he ordered Col Nakaguma's Fourth Regiment to move east to the Matanikau and take over from Oka. Col Nakaguma went on ahead of his troops to confer with Oka, expecting to find him on the other side of the river. As customary, however, Oka's command post was as far from the scene of any potential action as possible, Nakaguma finding him in a ravine well over a mile from his front. To justify his discretion, Oka painted a dismal picture for Nakaguma—so much so that when the latter's troops arrived he ordered them to stay on the west bank with only a few hundred to cross over.

By a miserable stroke of fortune that very day, the Americans made a bold attack at the river mouth, and within 24 hours had completely seized the east bank. When Nakaguma phoned this to Maruyama, the division commander was beside himself. He told Nakaguma to retake the position in an immediate night attack. It was all very well for Maruyama and his well-fed staff officers to talk of an "immediate" attack, grumbled

Nakaguma, but there on the spot he had no communication, for his units had been scattered by the paralyzing suddenness of the enemy assault. It was already 0230—to counterattack was impossible.

Several days later the bulk of the Americans withdrew, but they left behind about a thousand men who promptly erected barbed wire barriers and pillboxes at the sandspit, over which the Jap heavy equipment, artillery and supplies were to have rolled. It was most regrettable.

The troops pouring down from Rabaul had little idea that things were so bad; their morale was superb. Only two weeks ago, it had been announced over the radio, "Our submarines have finally entered the Atlantic Ocean. The movement of our navy from the Pacific—which it has subjugated—is significant, and has been a tremendous shock to England and America."

This was a little hard to swallow in view of the savage American air attacks against convoys moving south, but it was probably the enemy's death throes.

The pep talks their officers gave the men was the first hint of trouble, for their leaders were very frank in warning them of difficulty, and in pointing out the strategic importance of the battle.

Hyakutake had told his commanders and staff that Singapore paled in significance to Guadalcanal. Of course, it was no secret that he felt Gen Yamashita had gotten entirely too much publicity from the Malayan push, but a glance at the map was enough to convince them of the truth of Hyakutake's words.

The troops heard more disquieting rumors when they talked to the men of the Kawaguchi Brigade after landing. It had always been a well known fact that the American was basically a coward, unable to bear hardship, and worshipping only the material luxuries which could be seen in American movies. American tactics, their manuals had taught them, disdained the spiritual element exemplified by Japanese doctrines, and relied on materiel to keep the enemy at arm's length. Yankees feared cold steel.

But the Lunga Point veterans told them that these Americans were fierce brutal murderers known as marines. Chosen from the scum of the prisons and insane asylums of America for love of killing, they were so dreaded in the U.S.A. that they were invariably kept under guard there lest they lash out in uncontrollable massacre.

There was no type of atrocity they would not commit. One survivor of the Tenaru described how three comrades had advanced towards the marine lines waving a white flag. The marines machine-gunned all three before they had a chance to throw their hand grenades. The battle yells, once so unnerving to the enemy, now only provoked a return torrent of profanity and vulgarity.

If any soldier had ever secretly entertained thoughts of surrender, such stories erased such thoughts. Officers promised their men that after the American capitulation, the marines would be punished. All would be marched to the hallowed ground at the mouth of the Tenaru, where Ichiki and his heroic band had been slaughtered. After a ceremony, the Japanese would put them to the sword.

Despite these horror stories, Maruyama had full confidence in his men, for his Second Division was one of Japan's finest—founded many years before by the Emperor Shintake. Recruited from the Sandai District of Honshu, its soldiers were considered dull yokels by some, but nonetheless honest and diligent. After long Manchurian service it was brought back to Japan in 1941 to become part of Lt-Gen Hitoshi Imamura's SIXTEENTH ARMY, then being formed for the invasion of Java. After this campaign, it spent several months doing garrison duty until the American invasion of Guadalcanal necessitated its transfer to the Solomons. Speed was so essential that part of the division was transported on cruisers, the rest coming on in transports.

The first two weeks of October found the division being landed, as well as the service units, tanks, and heavy artillery of the SEVENTEENTH ARMY. As soon as the 150-mm howitzers were ashore they were brought up to shell the airfields (the Americans had now built another just west of the Lunga River). Although they quickly put the new one out of commission, the failure of Nakaguma's men to secure the Matanikau River crossing prevented the artillery men from advancing to where they could stop activity on the main airfield.

The navy, however, helped to make up for this in a succession of terrific night bombardments. The best was on the 13th, when the battleship *Haruna*—which the Americans had "sunk" in their lying newspapers—and the battleship *Kongo*, plus three cruisers and six destroyers, had shelled the airfield for almost three hours.

The bulk of the Naval Air Force had now been concentrated at Rabaul for the sole purpose of neutralizing Lunga airfield. The Americans had few planes, but it had to be admitted that they used them skillfully. The Imperial communiques daily claimed vast numbers of them shot down, but the men could see many more of their own planes shot down than were admitted. It was most puzzling how the enemy kept the airfield going. Observers could watch the Americans race out with trucks to fill in the bomb craters with dirt while the bombers were still overhead.

As psychological support, all of the homeland's short-wave propaganda was beamed on the marines. It was really most clever, particularly the "Zero Hour." Little Orphan Annie, after playing several Yankee jazz records, would remind the marines of the hopelessness of their cause, hint at the faithlessness of their wives and sweethearts, and try to stir up homesickness by recalling to them the memories of beefsteaks and pies.

With Little Orphan Annie, bombers, artillery, and battleships, the softening up was well under way when Hyakutake arrived on the 17th to assume personal command. His plan had been prepared at Rabaul, but changes in the situation, particularly the regrettable action at the Matanikau, necessitated alterations.

Hyakutake leaned heavily on his G-2, LtCol Matsumoto. In making his estimate of the situation, the latter had been somewhat handicapped by the failure of any marines to surrender, but the observation posts atop Mambulo virtually looked down the throats of the Americans. The enemy couldn't move a truck, a plane, or a Higgins boat without its being spotted through powerful telescopes. The Americans had become more skillful in concealing patrols, but there were few large troops movements that weren't followed, and the day-to-day progress in the construction of barbed wire barriers, antitank barricades, and gun positions was noted. Aerial photographs, Navy reports on enemy coast defense guns, and captured documents helped Matsumoto round out the picture.

He decided an entire division was defending the Lunga Point area by a continuous line of barbed wire, trenches, and pillboxes, with a battalion holding the advanced outpost position along the east bank of the Matanikau. Although captured organization tables of a marine division showed it to contain about 17,000 men, reports by Col Oka and MajGen Kawaguchi made it clear that at least 7000 marines had been annihilated. Thus, against only 10,000 marines, Hyakutake with his 25,000 would have better than a two-to-one quantitative superiority, in addition to the overwhelming spiritual superiority inherent in the Japanese soldier.

Hyakutake decided to split his army into two task forces. One, under MajGens Ito and Sumiyoshi, would assault the enemy battalion's positions at the Matanikau, while the other, under Gen Maruyama, would cut a secret trail well to the south of Mambulo, then strike north and launch the main attack over the same ground as had Kawaguchi in September. Since the Western Force was already in position, it was to wait until Maruyama's force had crossed the mountains to a position south of the airfield, then the attacks would be launched simultaneously.

Hyakutake had hoped that Maruyama would be in position by the 20th, but it became apparent he was moving slower than expected. This was very annoying, and the impatient Hyakutake finally decided to go ahead with the Matanikau attack, reasoning that to launch this blow might suck the enemy's reserves westwards, leaving only a thin crust around the airfield for Maruyama to break through.

It was planned that Oka's regiment would cross the Matanikau by the Nippon Bridge on the night of the 21st, then turn northwards and attack the battalion flank. At the same time Nakaguma's Fourth Regiment, with the 1st Independent Tank Company in the van, would force a crossing of the sandspit. All of Gen Sumiyoshi's massed artillery would support the attack.

Just about everything went wrong except the guns, which fired on schedule, but as soon as tanks approached the sandspit the lead one was knocked out by an American gun concealed on the other side of the river. Just as the enemy's artillery began to open up, a message came through from Hyakutake's headquarters calling off the attack. Col Oka, as usual, was about 24 hours behind schedule.

The 21st had been a bad day, but there had been few losses, and by the evening of the 23d everything would be ready for a really coordinated attack, for Oka had finally crossed the Nippon bridge. This time the assault would be pressed home at all costs—Hyakutake made that quite clear, especially to Col Oka, with whom he was extremely irritated. The latter was ordered to attack the southern flank in the afternoon, rather than at dusk when the other units were to attack. Hyakutake considered this rather clever. If Oka was as tardy as usual and didn't attack until the others did, well and good; if he did the unusual and struck at the appointed time the enemy would be diverted away from the river mouth upon which the main blow would fall. At 1800, Gen Sumiyoshi would concentrate the fire of all his heavy artillery on the enemy positions in a violent 10 minute bombardment, then the Fourth Regiment would drive across the sandspit behind Capt Maeda's twelve 17-ton tanks.

As the sun slowly went down, Nakaguma's men crawled through the trenches they had dug up to the very banks of the Matanikau, and put their machine-guns in position. Antitank and 70-mm gun crews wheeled their pieces up to camouflaged spots. Not a sound was made, for while more than 2000 men were creeping through the coconut grove to the river, on the other side the marines could be seen chatting and smoking by their fox-holes. By the time twilight was waning, the entire force was ready to pounce, the tanks within 100 yards of the spot over which they would race to break through the marine positions. On the hills to the west 75-mm, 105-mm, and 15-mm guns and howitzers were zeroed on the mouth of the Matanikau, the battery commanders waiting at their phones for the signal to fire.

Suddenly, as a red parachute flare went off, the bombardment began. Machine-guns, grenade dischargers, antitank and 70-mm guns joined in with the artillery. The tanks moved to their jump-off positions, the noise of their motors drowned out by the explosion of the shells. The American machine-guns opened up, and their mortars began to fire, but it was too late, because the lead tank, with the courageous Capt Maeda in com-mand, lumbered out onto the spit, turned, and with the throttle wide open, raced towards the enemy pillbox at the other end. In the light of the American flares, the men could see it tear right through the barbed wire entanglements. There was a roar of "banzais" as it crunched down the top of the pillbox. With the other tanks roaring across the spit behind him, Maeda quickly wheeled his tank to the left, got out onto the beach and raced down the enemy's flank. Just then, a marine fanatic left his foxhole and thrust a grenade in the tracks before Maeda could depress his machine-guns to stop him. The explosion of the grenade threw the tank out of control. No sooner had Maeda gotten it going again than an enemy half-track antitank gun, half concealed in the jun-gle, fired at him. Maeda swung his tank out into the surf in a wild effort to evade it, but the next shot hit home.

Within a few moments similar disaster struck the other 11 tanks and they became blazing wrecks. As the crews, screaming in agony from their burns, crawled out of the turrets to escape, the marines ripped them with machine-guns.

But the officers kept yelling for the men to go forward. Several, who had fashioned little camouflage rafts of twigs and leaves, slipped down through the marsh weeds and began swimming slowly across. There were fiendish shouts of glee from the brutal Yankee dogs as a fusillade of rifle bullets tore into these heroes before they had gone a few feet. The marines began to increase their artillery and mortar fire. It was every man for himself now, but there was no escape, for a curtain of heavy artillery fire was falling to the rear, cutting off any retreat.

When morning came, a few survivors found the coconut grove strewn with the mangled remains of comrades. In the stagnant river, two crocodiles lazily snapped at the half-awash bodies of the scouts, while on the sandpit the marines could be seen gaily talking away as they searched through blackened tank hulls for souvenirs.

Where had Oka been all this time?

He was supposed to have attacked the ridge forming the enemy's southern flank early the afternoon of the 23d, but Gen Ito, his immediate superior, scanned the ridge all day without seeing any evidence of the marines being disturbed in their chores. As H-hour for the Fourth Regiment drew near, Ito frantically radioed Oka to hurry and launch his attack. Oka sent only evasive replies, promising the attack any minute.

The minutes gave way to hours. Came the suicidal attack of the Fourth and not so much as a shot from Oka's direction. All during the night, as the full force of the marine artillery concentrated on Nakaguma's men, there was silence on the marines' southern flank.

Ito, now wild with rage—for he had to account in turn to Hyakutake—radioed message after message the morning of the 24th demanding an immediate attack, but every time he looked at the southern ridge he could see nothing but marines calmly digging entrenchments. At length he received a message from Oka stating that a lookout position had been "captured" on the northwestern slopes of Mambulo.

Oka had evidently tried to burn the candle at both ends. After crossing the Matanikau, instead of keeping his unit in an assembly area close to the enemy ridge, he had marched southwards towards Mt Austen, in order to be as far away as possible from the American mortars until the time for the attack. The official report finally submitted to Ito completely whitewashed this wretched performance, possibly as it was written by Oka himself. It described how the "regimental commander" (Oka) urged his unit along through incredible hardships, clearing a road through "jungle, precipice, and ravine" so that the attack could be launched at 1300 of the 23d. The report then said that due to the "confusing terrain and extremely sharp gullies," progress was slowed up a bit, despite the example set by the troops' fighting commander.

At length, at dusk of the 24th, some 29 hours late, Oka finally had his battalions at the foot of the ridge. After scaling the ridge, each battalion would head for one of the prominent hills indicated on the operations maps.

The attack started off quite successfully, and the men poured over the ridge, but when the puzzled battalion commanders looked around for the hills they were supposed to take, all they could make out was a succession of labyrinthine coral ridges—all the same height. By the time the enemy began to react with violent firing the units were completely lost—some firing on each other in the confusion.

Oka, after having given his commanders one of his "pep talks," remained in the ravine south of the ridge. But when the enemy mortars began to open up and it appeared that the issue might be in doubt, Oka hastily abandoned his command post and trotted back to the safety of the Nippon Bridge, several miles away.

Disgusted with Oka, and with the enemy threatening to defeat each unit in detail in the coral ridges, the battalion commanders began to withdraw to the ridge. When daylight came many of the units found themselves completely exposed in the grassy ravines with no conceal-ment. Then the marines, few of whom could be seen, opened up with devastating rifle fire. The final blow came when about 200 marines charged down from the ridges to the north, bayonets flashing and screaming weird yells and whoops. It was terrifying.

Now recovered from his fright, Oka submitted the final report. He had to admit that against 281 dead or missing of his own command, only 200 marines had been definitely killed, although one had been captured while semi-conscious and was "disposed of on the spot."

The attack on the Matanikau had been a failure because of piecemeal assaults, the failure of Sumiyoshi's artillery to neutralize the marine positions, and above all, the pusillanimous action of Oka. But while no ground had been gained and the Fourth Regiment annihilated, there was evidence that the enemy had moved reserves from Lunga Point west to the Matanikau. Hyakutake rationalized that perhaps the Matanikau attack might not be such a failure after all if Maruyama could break through a weakened enemy line when he assaulted the airfield.

Two weeks previously, Gen Maruyama, then at Kokumbona, had ordered Capt Oda to take his engineer unit and blaze a trail from Kokumbona around the southern side of Mambulo to the spot south of the airfield from which the main attack would be launched. After spend-ing an entire day going over aerial photographs of the area with Col Matsumoto, Oda and his group set off. By 14 Oct they had descended the sharp cliffs bordering the upper Matanikau, crossed the river, and reached the base of Mambulo. Cheery messages were sent to Maruyama informing him that there was only another day's work to cut the trail to the Lunga.

But the next day found the group reaching one ridge only to find another directly ahead—and none on the map. An argument broke out between Capt Oda and 1stLt Hisatomi, one insisting the best route was due south, the other southeast. It now appeared that Mambulo was not the one single height the maps had indicated, but rather a confusing mass of ravines and cliffs.

Aerial photographs showed only fleecy clouds, and solid jungle.

However, after many false starts, and considerable bickering between Oda and Hisatomi, the Lunga was reached on the 17th.

Back at Kokumbona, Maruyama was under the impression that everything was well, principally because of Oda's optimistic reports. Accordingly he ordered his main force to advance over the trail (now named "Maruyama Road") with five days' rations. This didn't allow much leeway but Maruyama saw little sense in burdening his men—after the battle he would feed his men from captured marine stocks.

Until they reached the headwaters of the Matanikau, the main body made fairly good progress, but when they reached the cliffs towering over the river the trouble began. Oda's lightly-equipped trail blazers had been able to crawl down them by grasping the tufts of grass growing from the coral, but the men of the main force were burdened with not only 50-odd pounds of personal equipment but machine-guns, grenade dischargers, and ammunition. There were no mules and all of the division's horses had been left at Rabaul, so the heavy ordnance—the 37-mm antitank guns, 70-mm and 75-mm field pieces had to be manhandled. The only way to negotiate these cliffs was to lower the field pieces by ropes. Such a slow process was impossible in daylight with the American planes circling overhead like vultures, so most of the difficult crossings had to be at night.

It soon became apparent that everyone must go on half-rations. The toll on the men had been heavy—they were getting practically no sleep, and their muscles burned, but their officers set them a splendid example. They ate no more than the men, and, save for some of the senior officers, carried machine-guns and ammunition like the privates. These men of Japan's finest regiments had not tasted earlier defeat, and they were imbued with a sacred mission. Often, when it seemed impossible to advance a step further without collapsing, the officers would lead their own men in the singing of the "Kima Ga Yo"—the national anthem. Facing in the direction of the homeland the men, tears streaming down their cheeks, would sing as loud as they could, and let Yankee patrols be damned.

Often had they heard the Imperial Rescript of the Emperor Meiji, but never under more impressive circumstances than when it was read to them in the Mambulo jungles before they began the day's march. The old familiar words, always inspiring, took on new meaning as they were punctuated by the eerie calls of the cockatoos overhead. . . . "I am your Commander-in-Chief, you are my strong arms. Whether I shall adequately fulfill my duty to the Ancestors depends on your fidelity. If you unite with me, our courage and power shall illuminate the whole earth . . ."

By the 20th, the forward units had finally crossed the Lunga, but so far upstream there was still six miles of jungle between them and the airfield. Sill, the worst of the 35-mile trek was over, and the enemy had apparently not yet perceived the move. Since there appeared to be a strong possibility that the Americans might capitulate even before the attack jumped off, Maruyama instructed his units on the 21st that in case the marines forwarded a surrender proposal they were to be told that they must lay down their arms immediately and leave their supplies and equipment intact. The enemy commander, a MajGen Vandegrift, according to the American press, was to walk to the mouth of the Matanikau and formally surrender to Gen Hyakutake.

Maruyama had planned that the main effort would be made by the 29th Regiment northward over the same ridge that Kawaguchi had attacked in September. On the left, the 16th Regiment would drive toward Lunga Point along the west bank of the Lunga, while over on the right Gen Kawaguchi, back once more at his old stamping grounds, would push through with a force of about 2500 to the eastern end of the airfield. If all went well, 1000 men from Kokumbona would sneak along the coast in barges and make a direct landing at Lunga Point, landings being a Jap specialty.

On the basis of the flood of optimistic reports, Maruyama expected that his units would be ready to attack by late afternoon of the 22d, but he finally realized that they were far behind schedule, and postponed the assault to the 23d. From the mountains by the upper Lunga the airfield had seemed tantalizingly near, but down in the steamy jungle ravines the men were barely moving. Heavy rains had churned the ground into a quagmire, and the trails were so slippery the slightest grade called for ropes. Came the 23d and the force was still bogged down. Again Maruyama had to postpone H-hour—this time until 1700 of the 24th.

It's understandable that the 29th should have been chosen to launch the main attack, for in all of Japan no regiment's colors were more honored. Even the Yankee LtCol Warren Clear, who had spent many weeks with it as an observer prior to the Greater East Asia War, had written of how it had made a practice march of 122 miles in 72 hours and double-timed at the end of it.[2]

In an order of the day, the commander, Col Furumiya, had exhorted his men to push without stint for the honor of their regimental colors and the great traditions it represented. But struggle as they might, they could not advance quickly enough. When H-hour came, the lead units had become hopelessly lost. An officer patrol was sent forward to spot the enemy positions, but could find none. The sickening realization that they were still miles to the south of the airfield was not helped by a torrential downpour that made the going even more difficult. Furumiya had had two battalions advancing abreast and one in reserve, but this tidy formation became thoroughly mixed up as each unit hacked trails in what they thought was the right direction. Finally, just before midnight of the 25th, 31 hours late, the forward units ran into the enemy positions. There was no artillery fire to support them, and the units were disorganized. As soon as the enemy learned of the attack they began firing heavy concentrations of machine-gun, mortar and artillery fire. Furumiya's companies couldn't mass for bayonet charges because of the shells.

The men were not advancing as they should. Determined to inspire them, Furumiya with a group of men and the regimental colors rushed the enemy barbed wire, his Samurai sword flashing. The men saw their commander break through the American line but a fresh burst of fire stopped them dead when they followed him. Attempt after attempt was made, but the assaults grew weaker as the artillery grew fiercer.

When morning came, Maruyama found that while the 29th had been almost cut to pieces, the regiments on either side hadn't even made contact with the Americans.

There seemed little chance that a continuation of the attack could have any real success. The temptation to withdraw and conserve the unit's strength for a later attack was strong. But it was not in the tradition of Bushido for a Japanese warrior to abandon a course once taken; Maruyama radioed Hyakutake that all was well, and that the airfield was as good as captured. He meanwhile ordered increased daylight reconnaissance in preparation for another attack that night.

But Maruyama, as he well knew himself, was butting against a wall. He had lost his precious weapon—surprise. Officers grumbled that to attack against fixed defenses without heavy artillery support was suicidal. Defeatism had begun to seep through to the tired and hungry men. The Division motto had once seemed glorious—"Remember that Death is lighter than a feather, but that Duty is heavier than a mountain." They would do their duty all right, but death had lost its attractiveness in the bodies of comrades, decomposing in the sun.

The final attack didn't even get as far as the first one—the punch was gone. The enemy lines in front of the 29th Regiment had been strengthened, while over on the right, Gen Kawaguchi, taught discretion by his experience in the same area, saw no reason for another useless slaughter. Before dawn broke, Maruyama realized that he could no longer delay a retreat.

Meanwhile, his earlier and somewhat premature victory dispatches, embellished by each higher headquarters as they were transmitted back to Japan, were taking effect. There was rejoicing throughout the Empire as it was announced that the airfield had been seized and that the American capitulation was expected. In propaganda, Radio Tokyo proclaimed to the marines, "As a result of the battle . . . you are now marooned, with no communications. You are deprived of arms and ammunition, and your resistance is leading you only to death!" The point was further driven home to the Yankees by a comparison to their national game, "The score stands U. S. Navy—0; Japan—21, with the Japanese deep in American territory, 10 yards to go. Coach Roosevelt passes up and down chain-smoking cigarettes. A pass is knocked down. America calls time out and Ghormley is pulled from the game. The Rising Sun cheers loudly for Coach Tojo. Roosevelt sends in Halsey to call signals. Another pass is called, but the ball is fumbled on the one-yard line, and the heavy favorites, the U.S., are in a bad way as the gun signals the end of the first half."

The Second Division's attack on the airfield had been a bloody failure; but even in defeat honor could be saved. Furumiya and the regimental colors of the 29th were still missing—they had to be found at all costs. Hyakutake himself ordered that no effort be spared to find him. On the night of the 26th, Maruyama sent out a six-man officer patrol. They returned empty-handed. The next night, even though the retreat had begun, a still larger group of 10 went out . . . again, no luck.

Only a few hundred yards separated the searching parties from

Furumiya, but it might as well have been miles, for American barbed wire lay between them. The night of the first attack, Furumiya's group had penetrated the lines, but when dawn broke the next morning he found the gap closed by American reinforcements.

There were only nine left with him—Capt Suzuki, Lt Ono, WO Kobayashi, and six men. They hadn't been spotted by the enemy yet, but although each had draped himself with vines and leaves it seemed that only a miracle would prevent the enemy from stumbling across them.

At first it had seemed that there was only one course—suicide. But as Furumiya thought the matter over several objections arose. The colors had to be destroyed. Burning was the only safe means of disposing of them, but the smoke of a fire would attract attention. To bury the colors would be unsatisfactory, for the Americans were doing a prodigious amount of digging and might easily uncover them. Death would be sweet, reasoned Furumiya, but clearly his duty lay in escaping with the colors. Lt Ono and two soldiers were dispatched to find an escape gap through the lines, with instructions to report back as soon as they had found it.

While awaiting Ono, Furumiya peered through his veil of foliage at the activity of the Americans in the little plain in front of him. He marveled at the way they went about their business efficiently and without much talking. He was particularly interested in the disposition of the enemy defenses. The machine-gun nests were spaced about 50 yards apart and no one seemed to stand by them. Furumiya concluded that the machine-guns were fired by electricity, and directed by remote control.

When eight hours had passed without the return of Ono's group, loyal old WO Kobayashi crawled off alone to find them. But when night fell and even he had not returned, Furumiya again considered suicide. The circumstances almost demanded it—he had failed. Tears came to his eyes. Here he was, the commander of one of the Emperor's finest regiments, miserably hiding in the enemy's camp! He looked at his Samurai sword. Was the blade that served his ancestors to lie rusting in this jungle or be soiled by souvenir-hunting Yankees?

Suddenly it came to him—he would not slink through the American lines; he would attack! Happy at this thought, he drafted a complete regimental operation order for his five men. H-hour would be 0440, the "objective" a point in the line 20 meters east of the spot where they had originally penetrated it. The group would advance silently until they reached the front line, then they would rush. In the event of casualties, he drew up a list designating his successors as regimental commander.

A little after midnight, the six men crawled up to the edge of the jungle. Between the jungle and the front line there was a grass-covered ridge they had to cross. In the moonlight their silhouettes could be spotted by the enemy sentries, so they crept along the edge of the jungle. When clouds obscured the moon, they would dash across the open space. So skillfully did they do so that, although they passed several American positions, no alarm was given. But when it became daylight, they were still 100 yards from the lines.

All during the next day, they hid in a clump of vegetation, not daring to move, for they were next to a mortar emplacement. Hunger and thirst had become almost unbearable, particularly when they could smell American cooking not far way.

Although once again on the verge of suicide, Furumiya decided on taking one more crack at escaping. This time they would break up into two-man groups, each going off in different directions. They ended up, however, by moving together and this time they were fired upon by the enemy

With a searching party combing the jungle for them, it was now obvious that escape was impossible. Furumiya asked Capt Suzuki if he was ready to kill himself. Capt Suzuki nodded his head gravely. Furumiya slowly scrawled a note to Gen Maruyama, apologizing for his failure, and explaining that he would take the regimental colors and tear it to bits. Tearfully, he began ripping the flag to strips, tearing each strip into pieces. A searching party thrashed through the bush. Frantically, Furumiya threw leaves over the brilliant red and white scraps of silk, and ground others into the dirt. Capt Suzuki had drawn his pistol and was waiting quietly.

It was better this way. Like the men of the SEVENTEENTH ARMY now struggling back to the Matanikau, Furumiya knew he and his men had been representing the honor of Japan in a battle whose decision would be final and irrevocable, and he knew they had lost. Better that he die now and join his ancestors at the Yasukuni Shrine than taste defeat again. As Capt Suzuki raised his pistol to Furumiya's temple, the regimental commander scrawled his last words to Maruyama. . . . "The mission of a Japanese warrior is to serve his Emperor! "

1. Reprinted with permission from the *Marine Corps Gazette* (July and August, 1945).
2. "Close-up of the Jap Fighting Man"—LtCol Warren J. Clear, USA; *Infantry Journal,* Nov 1942.

Appendix B

Pacific Fleet Chain of Command

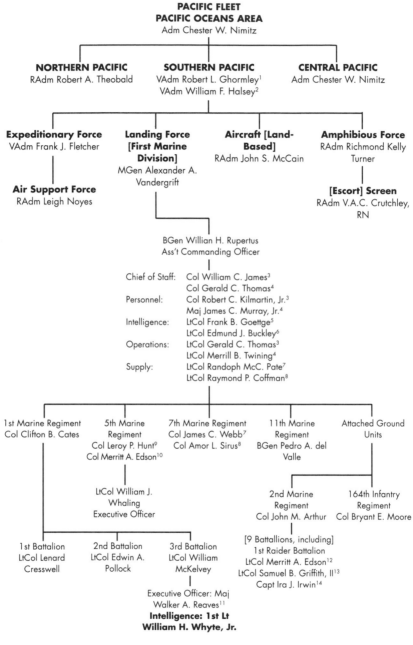

PACIFIC FLEET
PACIFIC OCEANS AREA
Adm Chester W. Nimitz

NORTHERN PACIFIC
RAdm Robert A. Theobald

SOUTHERN PACIFIC
VAdm Robert L. Ghormley[1]
VAdm William F. Halsey[2]

CENTRAL PACIFIC
Adm Chester W. Nimitz

Expeditionary Force
VAdm Frank J. Fletcher

Air Support Force
RAdm Leigh Noyes

Landing Force
[First Marine
Division]
MGen Alexander A.
Vandergrift

Aircraft [Land-
Based]
RAdm John S. McCain

Amphibious Force
RAdm Richmond Kelly
Turner

[Escort] Screen
RAdm V.A.C. Crutchley,
RN

BGen Willian H. Rupertus
Ass't Commanding Officer

Chief of Staff:	Col William C. James[3]
	Col Gerald C. Thomas[4]
Personnel:	Col Robert C. Kilmartin, Jr.[3]
	Maj James C. Murray, Jr.[4]
Intelligence:	LtCol Frank B. Goettge[5]
	LtCol Edmund J. Buckley[6]
Operations:	LtCol Gerald C. Thomas[3]
	LtCol Merrill B. Twining[4]
Supply:	LtCol Randoph McC. Pate[7]
	LtCol Raymond P. Coffman[8]

1st Marine Regiment
Col Clifton B. Cates

5th Marine
Regiment
Col Leroy P. Hunt[9]
Col Merritt A. Edson[10]

7th Marine Regiment
Col James C. Webb[7]
Col Amor L. Sirus[8]

11th Marine
Regiment
BGen Pedro A. del
Valle

Attached Ground
Units

LtCol William J.
Whaling
Executive Officer

2nd Marine
Regiment
Col John M. Arthur

164th Infantry
Regiment
Col Bryant E. Moore

1st Battalion
LtCol Lenard
Cresswell

2nd Battalion
LtCol Edwin A.
Pollock

3rd Battalion
LtCol William
McKelvey

[9 Battalions, including]
1st Raider Battalion
LtCol Merritt A. Edson[12]
LtCol Samuel B. Griffith, II[13]
Capt Ira J. Irwin[14]

Executive Officer: Maj
Walker A. Reaves[11]
Intelligence: 1st Lt
William H. Whyte, Jr.

1 June to 18 October 1942
2 After 18 October 1942
3 To 21 September
4 After 21 September
5 Missing in Action 12 August
6 After 12 August
7 To 21 October
8 After 21 October

9   Until 19 September
10 After 19 September
11 Until 25 September
12 To 20 September
13 Commanded 21 September to 27 September when he
    was Wounded in Action
14 After 27 September

Index

Americans: character of, 31, 94–95; losses by, 79
Amphibious warfare, 13–14, 16–17
Aola Bay, Guadalcanal, 82
Arthur, John M., 82, 140
Australia, 24, 88–91

Baldwin, Hanson, 75
Barnett, 23
Bartsch, William H., 48–49
Basilone, John, 78
Beatty, David, 5
Blank walls, 108
Bootleggers, 6–7
Bougainville, 24
Brandywine Valley, 3–4
Brisbane, Australia, 88–89
Bryant Park, 109
Buckley, Edmund J., 54, 140
Bushido, 30, 101
Butler, Smedley Darlington "Old Gimlet Eye," 12–13

Callaghan, Daniel J., 26, 81–82
Cameron, Bill, 8
Canberra, 32
Cape Esperance, battle of, 67
Carlson, Evans F., 22, 65, 83
Catalano, sergeant, 11–12
Cates, Clifton B., 29, 140; on battle of Matanikau spit, 74–75; at battle of

Tenaru, 40; on firepower, 100–101; on Japanese, 30, 49, 60–61, 97; on Marines after Guadalcanal, 86; on National Guard, 79–80
Champagne, Joseph D. R., 73
Chicago, 32–33
Chinese, 22, 31, 38, 83
Churchill, Winston, 14
Clapp, Lady, 89
Clear, Warren, 77–78, 135
Clemens, W. F. Martin, 35, 114
Cluster development, 107–8
Coastwatchers, 35, 44
Coffman, Raymond P., 140
Conservation, Whyte and, 107–8
Conte Biancomo, 91
Coral Sea, battle of, 24
Cram, Jack, 68
Cresswell, Lenard "Charlie," 23–24, 34, 40, 53–54, 140
Crutchley, Victor A. C., 26, 32, 140

Daly, Daniel J. "Fighting Dan," 12
del Valle, Pedro A., 74, 100, 140
Diamond, Lee, 40
Diamond, Lou, 91–92
Dix, private, 56
Duhamel, Arthur C., 35
Dumas, captain, 42–43

Easements, Whyte and, 107–8

Eastern Solomons, battle of, 44
Edson, Merritt A. "Red Mike," 22, 27,
    45, 59, 82, 140; and battle of Edson's
    Ridge, 50–52; and battle of
    Matanikau spit, 65, 67
Edson's Ridge, battle of, 22, 45–52
Elizabeth II, queen of Great Britain, 36
Ellis, Earl H. "Pete," 13–14, 16, 34
Eniwetok, 13
Evans, Walker, 104

Fiji, 26
Firepower: American, 74, 97, 100–101;
    Japanese on, 79, 101
First Marine Battalion, 1
Fleet Training Publication No. 167,
    *Landing Operations Doctrine, U.S.
    Navy,* 14, 23, 34
Fletcher, Frank Jack, 26, 32, 44, 140
Fortune magazine, 104
Frank, Richard B.: on air battles, 82; on
    American plans, 50; on battle of
    Tassafaronga, 84; on bombardment
    of Guadalcanal, 68; on defense of
    Henderson Field, 51; on Geiger, 100;
    on Guadalcanal, 86–87; on Ichiki,
    38; on Kuma Battalion, 48; on maps,
    70; on marine numbers, 33; on Terzi
    mission, 47
Furimiya, colonel, 78–79, 136–38

Gage, Gerry, 89
Gallipoli, 14
Geiger, Roy S., 100
Ghormley, Robert L., 24, 26, 32, 68,
    102, 140
Gibbons, Floyd, 12
Goettge, Frank B., 25, 54, 140
Griffith, Samuel B. II, 18, 140
Griswold, Whitney, 106
Guadalcanal: air battles over, 43–44,
    49, 82; battle of Tenaru, 36–45; bom-
    bardment of, 67–69; campaign, char-
    acteristics of, 30; confusion over

rivers on, 1, 26, 28; geography of, 25,
    27; historical evaluation of, 86–87,
    96–103; insignia for, 87; Japanese
    occupation of, 24–25, 29; Japanese
    view of, 97–99, 111–38; malaria on,
    71–72; Marine landing on, 27–36;
    natives of, 25, 34, 113; naval battles
    off, 32–33, 67, 81–82, 84; patrolling
    on, 53–62; socialization on, 43; U.S.
    defense of, 33–34; U.S. plans for, 24,
    26; Vandegrift on, 85; Whyte as
    instructor on, 93–103; winding
    down on, 81–87

Hagikaze, 39
Halsey, William F. "Bull," 69, 89, 140
Hartshorne, Joshua, 3
Haruna, 67, 127
Heinl, Robert D., 13
Hemphill, Alec, 2–3, 5
Hemphill, Dallett, 2, 5
Henderson Airfield, Guadalcanal, 29,
    43–44; and air battles, 82; battle of,
    46–52; completion of, 33
Higgins, Andrew Jackson, 16–17
Hiraide, captain, 124
Hisatomi, first lieutenant, 76, 97–99,
    133
Hodges, Eric, 104
Holcomb, Thomas, 31, 41
Hornet, 81
Hunt, George, 89, 91
Hunt, Leroy P., 29, 140
Hyakutake, Harukichi, 38, 69, 77, 82,
    96; Whyte's article on, 111–38

Ichiki Detachment, 44–45, 97, 99
Ichiki, Kiyono, 38–41, 116–18
Imamura, Hitoshi, 127
Individualism, 8, 19, 106–7
Irwin, Ira J., 140
Ishimoto, officer, 34–35, 113–15
Ishitari, major, 50, 120–21
Ito, major general, 75, 128, 131

James, William C., 140
Japan/Japanese: on American character, 31, 38–39, 94–95, 102, 126–27; and battle of Matanikau spit, 63–80; and battle of Tenaru, 36, 61, 97; documents and diaries captured from, 45, 60, 77, 84, 95, 97–99, 101–3; errors of, 30, 33, 77–78, 96, 100, 102–3; forces on Guadalcanal, 32, 38–39, 66, 115–17; losses of, 79–80, 97; malaria among, 71–72; and maps, 70; and Marine patrols, 53–62; morale of, 62, 123; navy of, 127; occupation of Guadalcanal, 24–25, 29, 34–35; plans of, 39, 44–45, 49–50, 70–71, 75–76; predictions regarding, 13; preparedness of, 60–61; as prisoners, 54–55, 95–96; propaganda of, 69–70, 128, 136; tactics of, 61–62; at Tulagi, 27; view of Guadalcanal, 97–99, 111–38
Japanese character, 2, 29–31, 41; Whyte as instructor on, 93–103
Jefferson amphibious tractor, 28

Kawaguchi Brigade, 99
Kawaguchi, Kiyotake, 44, 49–52, 71, 77, 118, 120–23, 134–36
Kilmartin, Robert C., Jr., 140
Kinkaid, Thomas, 26
Kirishima, 82
Knox, Frank, 22
Kobayashi, warrant officer, 79, 137
Kodoma, captain, 29, 37, 112–13, 115
Kokumbona, fake landing at, 64–65
Kokusho, Yukichi, 98
Kondo, superior private, 79
Kongo, 67, 127
Koro, 26
Koror, 14
Krulak, Victor H. "Brute," 16
Kuma Battalion, 48, 50–51

Lejeune, John A., 14, 16

MacArthur, Douglas, 88
Maeda, captain, 73, 129–30
Malaria, 71–72, 91
Maps, 1, 4, 8–9, 91, 109; of Guadalcanal, 25–28, 53–54
Marine Corps Gazette, Whyte's articles in, 103–5, 111–38
Marshall Islands, 13
Maruyama, Furimiya's note to, 79, 138
Maruyama, Masao, 66–67, 70, 76–77, 111, 125–29, 132–36
Matanikau spit, battle of, 63–80
Matsumoto, Hiroshi, 70, 111, 128
Maxwell, William E., 28–29
McCain, John, 26, 140
McCawley, 23, 26, 31
McKelvy, William N. "Wild Bill" (elder), 13, 42
McKelvy, William "Wild Bill," 18–19, 80, 140; and battle of Tenaru, 40; character of, 1–2, 18, 31, 42–43, 63–64, 103; and defense of Guadalcanal, 34; and defense of Henderson Field, 46–47; in evacuation, 85–86; and Kokumbona landing, 64–65; and maps, 53–54; Navy Cross, 59; and patrols, 57; and routine, 41–42; and Whyte, 23, 28, 40
McMillan, George, 17, 69
Melbourne, Australia, 89
Michener, James, 87
Midway, battle of, 24
Mikawa, Gunichi, 32–33, 37, 102
Mizuno, Eiji, 48
Moore, Bryant E., 68, 80, 140
Morison, Samuel Eliot, 84
Moskin, J. Robert, 14
Mount Austen, Guadalcanal, 27–29, 70
Murray, James C., Jr., 140
Musachi, 103

Nakaguma, colonel, 73–74, 125–26, 129
National Geographic Society, 108

National Guard, 68, 79–80
Navajo Indians, 91
New River, NC, 17
New Zealand, 22–24, 26
Nimitz, Chester, 66, 68, 69, 140
Noyes, Leigh, 140
Nuns, 35, 113–14

Observation, 105–6
Oda, captain, 76, 133
Ogawa, sergeant, 79
Oka, Akinosuku, 44, 49–52, 71, 75–76,
    96, 103, 119–25, 129, 131–32
Okimura, lieutenant commander, 29,
    112–13
Ono, lieutenant, 79, 137
The Organization Man (Whyte), 106–7
Organizations, 8
Oude-Engberink, Henry, 35

Pacific Fleet, chain of command in, 140
Paine, Del, 106
Palau, 44
Patch, Alexander M., 85
Pate, Randolph McC., 140
Peleliu Island, 14
Pell, Walden and Edith, 94
Polifka, Karl, 25
Pollock, Edwin A., 39, 140
Price, Eulalia, 7
Price, grandfather, 4
Price, grandmother, 4, 7
Price, Joe, 2, 4–7
Priests, 35, 113–14
Princeton University, 8
Puller, Lewis B. "Chesty," 65, 78
Putnam, captain, 64

Quantico, VA: Whyte as instructor at,
    93–103; Whyte as recruit at, 11–12,
    14–15

Rabaul, 24, 37
Raider battalions, 22
Reagan, Francis X., 47

Reaves, Walker A., 41, 140
Reed, Jack, 35
Richards, Pete, 68
Rivers, John, 40
Rockefeller, Laurance S., 107
Roosevelt, Franklin D., 22, 81
Rupertus, William H., 140
Russell Islands, 82
Ryujo, 44

St. Andrew's School, 3, 8, 19
Sakamoto, superior private, 79
Santa Cruz, battle of, 81
Sato, corporal, 79
Sato, Torajiro (captain), 39
Schmid, Albert A., 40
Scott, admiral, 81–82
Seabees, 82
Sendai Division, 66
Shoji, colonel, 71, 78, 83
Shoup, David, 83
Sirus, Amor L., 140
Slay, Ronnie, 89
Smith, Holland M. "Howlin' Mad," 17
Society of Mary, 35
Solomon Islands, 24–25; coastwatchers,
    35, 44
Solomons Island, MD, 16–17
Solow, Herbert, 104
South Dakota, 82
Spiritual warfare, Japanese on, 95, 101,
    126
Street Life Project, 108–9
Suicide, 30, 41, 101, 138
Sumiyoshi, major general, 128–29
Suzuki, captain, 79, 137–38

Takahara, lance corporal, 79
Tanaka, Raizo, 84, 101
Tassafaronga, battle of, 44, 84, 101
Taylor, Harold Kirby "Ramrod," 19–20,
    57–59
Tenaru, battle of, 36–45, 61, 75, 97
Terzi, Joseph A., 47–48
Theobald, Robert A., 140

Thomas, Gerald C., 140
Time, 81
Tojo, Hideki, 31
Tokunaga, Togo, 95
Torgerson, Harry, 51
Tregaskis, Richard, 46–47, 51, 75
Truk, 39
Truman, Harry, 17
Tulagi, 24, 27, 39
Turner, Richmond Kelly, 26, 31–32, 68, 85, 102, 140; and Aola Bay airfield, 82; and battle of Matanikau spit, 65–66; and defense of Henderson Airfield, 50–51
Twenty-ninth Regiment, 77–78
Twining, Merrill B. "Bill," 23, 29–30, 73, 140

U.S. Marine Corps: in Australia, 88–92; and battle of Tenaru, 37–45; character of, 12, 15–16, 18; insignia for Guadalcanal, 87; Japanese view of, 126–27; landing on Guadalcanal, 27–36; malaria in, 71–72; manual of, 16; nomenclature of, 22–23; numbers of, 12, 33; patrolling on Guadalcanal, 53–62; training in, 11–20; winding down on Guadalcanal, 81–87
U.S. Navy: and amphibious warfare, 17; battles off Guadalcanal, 32–33, 67, 81–82, 84; Joe Price in, 4–5

Vandegrift, Alexander Archer, 25, 33, 81, 103, 140; and battle of Edson's Ridge, 45; and battle of Matanikau spit, 65, 67; and battle of Tenaru, 40; on bombardment of Guadalcanal, 68–69; on Brisbane, 88–89; on closeness of Marines, 15–16; and defense of Guadalcanal, 33–34; and Edson, 22; on Guadalcanal campaign, 85; and Guadalcanal landing, 28–29; on Guadalcanal landing, 31; in New Zealand, 23; and other commanders,

26, 31–32; and patrols, 55; and reassignment of officers, 70–71; and Vouza, 36; and winding down, 82–83, 85
Vandegrift, Carson, 94
Vick School of Applied Merchandising, 8–10
Vouza, Jacob Charles, 35–36, 117

Wakisawa, corporal, 79
Walls, blank, 108
Walt, Lewis, 82
Washington, George, 3–4
Wasp, 35, 44
Webb, James C., 140
Wells, Erskine, 82
West Chester, PA, 2–3
West Point, 89
Whaling, William J., 55, 82, 140
Whyte, grandmother, 3
Whyte, Holly, Sr., 15
Whyte, Margaret, 15
Whyte, William H. "Holly," Jr.: and battle of Matanikau spit, 74–75; and battle of Tenaru, 37–45; childhood of, 1–10; at landing on Guadalcanal, 27–36; later life, 104–9; Marine training, 11–20; on patrol, 53–56; recuperation of, 88–92; shipping out, 21–26; as teacher, 91, 93–103; and Vouza, 35–36
Wike, corporal, 53
Williams, captain, 12
World War I, 12–13
Wright, Carleton, 84

Yale University, 106
Yamamoto, Isoroku, 24, 103, 111, 125
Yamashita, 126
Yamato, 103

"Zero Hour," 69–70, 128
Zimmerman, John, 67, 74